Advantage Play

Advantage Play

THE MANAGER'S GUIDE TO CREATIVE PROBLEM SOLVING

David Ben

KEY PORTER BOOKS

National Library of Canada Cataloguing in Publication Data

Ben, David
    Advantage play : the manager's guide to creative problem solving

ISBN: 1-55263-349-7

1. Problem solving. 2. Creative ability in business. 3. Selling. 4. Magic. I. Title.

HD53.B45 2001   650.1   C2001-900607-1

The publisher gratefully acknowledges the support of the Canada Council for the Arts and the Ontario Arts Council for its publishing program.

We acknowledge the financial support of the Government of Canada through the Book Publishing Industry Development Program (BPIDP) for our publishing activities.

Key Porter Books Limited
70 The Esplanade
Toronto, Ontario
Canada M5E 1R2

www.keyporter.com

Design: Jack Steiner
Electronic formatting: Jean Lightfoot Peters

Printed and bound in Canada

01 02 03 04 05 6 5 4 3 2 1

ARTIFICE

RUSE AND SUBTERFUGE

AT THE

CARD TABLE

A Treatise on the Science and Art of
Manipulating Cards

BY

S. W. ERDNASE

EMBRACING THE WHOLE CALENDAR OF SLIGHTS THAT
ARE EMPLOYED BY THE GAMBLER AND CON-
JURER, DESCRIBING WITH DETAIL AND ILLUS-
TRATION EVERY KNOWN EXPEDIENT,
MANOEUVRE AND STRATEGEM OF
THE EXPERT CARD HANDLER,
WITH OVER ONE HUNDRED
DRAWINGS FROM LIFE
BY M. D. SMITH

PRICE $2.00

PUBLISHED BY THE AUTHOR

In offering this book to the public the writer uses no sophistry as an excuse for its existence. The hypocritical cant of reformed (?) gamblers, or whining, mealy-mouthed pretensions of piety, are not foisted as a justification for imparting the knowledge it contains. To all lovers of card games it should prove interesting, and as a basis of card entertainment it is practically inexhaustible. It may caution the unwary who are innocent of guile, and it may inspire the crafty by enlightenment on artifice. It may demonstrate to the tyro that he cannot beat a man at his own game, and it may enable the skilled in deception to take a post-graduate course in the highest and most artistic branches of his vocation. But it will not make the innocent vicious, or transform the pastime player into a professional; or make the fool wise, or curtail the annual crop of suckers; but whatever the result may be, if it sells it will accomplish the primary motive of the author, as he needs the money.

S. W. ERDNASE

CONTENTS

CHAPTER ONE

The Expert at the Card Table

Man cannot change his temperament, and few care to control it. While the passion for hazard exists it will find gratification. We have neither grievance against the fraternity nor sympathy for so-called "victims." A varied experience has impressed us with the belief that all men who play for any considerable stakes are looking for the best of it.

S. W. ERDNASE

WELCOME TO THE OXBRIDGE CLUB, a private squash and fitness center for the financial elite of the City. On this particular night the members are staging a private tournament. Not just any tournament. For this particular tournament, the members have assembled the top, internationally ranked squash players for a little fun and relaxation. The players will compete against each other for prize money. The members will place large wagers on which player will emerge victorious. Hundreds of thousands of dollars will be lost and won—all in the spirit of fun.

As a prelude to the main event, poker tables are erected throughout the facility so the members can engage in a friendly game of cards. The minimum chip is worth a hundred dollars. Tens of thousands of dollars change hands. On this particular night, one player seems to be doing a little better than the others. He has only been a member for a few months. Tonight, however, he has recouped his membership fee in spades. It doesn't matter whether he deals the cards or not. Over the course of the evening, the cards just seem to fall in his favor. The members congratulate him on his luck and break from the game for the main event with the expectation that they will recoup their losses if not on the outcome of the squash game then the next time they meet at the card table. Unfortunately, they won't because the winner deceived them and he will do so again. Not by himself, but with a secret ally: the *mechanic* who was able to direct the course of play by dealing the winning hands to his partner. Cardsharps call this *Advantage Play.*

Now, pasteboard prestidigitation is not as easy as it appears. It requires persistence, diligence, attention to detail, observation, practice, teamwork, grace under pressure, management of resources—in fact all the attributes that business schools try to instill in their students and employers in their employees. It is a creative exercise that depends on one's ability to solve problems efficiently and effectively.

Although I am not a professional card hustler, I do practice the art of deception. I am a magician. I create and perform magic in theaters, on television, and at private performances throughout the world. Before I became a professional magician, however, I was a tax lawyer. Any doubts I may have had about the parallels between business and Advantage Play were erased by my sojourn in this world. Tax lawyers use the same problem-solving skills to shepherd their clients around Byzantine fiscal legislation as card hustlers do to orchestrate winning hands. Furthermore, both are creative exercises.

Now, I do not advocate cheating at cards or taxes. In addition to the legal issues, for me there are ethical standards that transcend the law. I firmly believe in playing by the rules. Having made the art of deception both my vocation and avocation, I am convinced that *principles* of deception can be separated from *the act* of deception and that anyone doing so becomes an *Advantage Player*—a player with an effective and legal advantage over the competition. The creative problem solver is an Advantage Player.

I first became interested in Advantage Play and its application to business when I was introduced to a small book published originally in 1902 entitled *Artifice, Ruse and Subterfuge at the Card Table*. It is subtitled "A Treatise on the Science and Art of Manipulating Cards." It is generally known today as "The Expert at the Card Table" or simply *Erdnase* after its author, S. W. Erdnase.* *Erdnase* is the first major work that describes in clinical detail the techniques employed to manipulate cards in play. It is not a mere exposé of the methods of the professional cardsharp but an actual guide designed to teach the requisite techniques so that the reader need not fall prey to such practitioners. It is a post-graduate course in the principles of deception. I learned from *Erdnase* a

---

* To differentiate between the author and the short form description of his book I will always describe the author as S. W. Erdnase and the book "Artifice, Ruse and Subterfuge at the Card Table" as *Erdnase*.

keen respect for the skills professionals must possess if they are to reach the pinnacle of their profession.

S. W. Erdnase himself is a mythic figure. Some scholars believe that S. W. Erdnase is an anagram for E.S. Andrews. Others believe that the name is a partial anagram for Milton Franklin Andrews, an itinerant cardsharp wanted in the United States for a variety of misdemeanors, including murder. Milton Franklin Andrews died in a murder-suicide in San Francisco in 1905. Whatever the true identity of the author, most experts agree that his little book would have fallen by the wayside if not for David Frederick Wingfield Verner.

Born in Ottawa in 1894, Verner obtained a paperback edition of *Erdnase* for twenty-five cents when he was eight years old. He had absorbed its contents by the time he was twelve. Verner moved to New York City in his early twenties and became Dai Vernon—the single most influential sleight of hand magician of the twentieth century. Vernon died in California in 1992, having contemplated, studied, analyzed, and interpreted during most of his life the contents of that very same book he picked up for a quarter on his way home from school. As a result of Vernon's work, *Erdnase* has remained in print since the day it was published and has become not only the seminal text for cardsharps but also a bible for magicians who perform sleight of hand. Who would have imagined that Vernon's initial twenty-five cent investment would have paid such dividends!

Vernon did, in fact, approach the book like a biblical scholar. His studies led him to two conclusions. First, *Erdnase* was much more than a series of techniques on how to cheat at cards. It was really a system—in essence, a management system—that one could employ to consistently and efficiently profit at the card table. It is not sufficient, for example, to be able to deal from the bottom of the pack. You must do more than that. First, you have to have the cards that you want to deal at the bottom. Second, you have to shuffle the cards without displacing the position of the cards that you want to control. Third, you have to have the deck cut by the person to your right and somehow insure that the cards that you have secreted at the bottom are not displaced during the cutting procedure. Fourth, you have to be able to deal the requisite cards in the order and to the person—be it yourself or a secret ally—you want to win without attracting suspicion. Finally, you have to do this under live conditions, with money on the table, and the potential consequences that may follow from every eye watching and analyzing your every movement. If you can manage all of this, you can win.

Despite the simple prose, *Erdnase* is filled with principles that apply to situations well beyond the scope of the card table. Unlike most magicians who are only interested in adding tricks to their repertoire, Vernon was interested in the principles inherent in this wisdom and how these principles can be applied to other aspects not contemplated by the initial creator. Vernon's own work was based on principles rather than specific techniques. This is not to disparage Vernon's technique, which was flawless, but to say that Vernon made sure his technique was built on a firm theoretical base. Hence, Vernon is responsible for importing not only the technical prowess of the professional cardsharp into the realm of the magician but also the management techniques that can be employed to profit from their advantage. By doing so he changed the way that problem solving is managed, magic is created, and the way it is performed.

I was introduced to *Erdnase* in my teens when I had the good fortune to study with another master magician, Ross Bertram. Eighteen years Vernon's junior, Bertram was also an authority on *Erdnase* and on sleight of hand. Bertram guided me line by line through the text. It inspired me then. It inspires me now twenty years later.

One of the joys of performing magic is that it brings me into contact with new people, places, and experiences. And even though the world of the stage appears to be far removed from the world of the corporate executive, the difference in application is only an illusion. They are one and the same. Stated simply: success comes to people who can solve problems. So, I am going to introduce you to the *Principles of Deception*—the theoretical base for problem solving in the real world—the equivalent of the high-stakes poker game in which the only way to succeed is to know how to win. They are drawn not only from *Erdnase* but also from my own experience in creating and performing and watching and working with people who are persistent and diligent and display grace under pressure.

Just as it takes the Advantage Player many years to become proficient, so too it takes a great deal of time and effort before these Principles of Deception become encoded in your brain. When I first started studying sleight of hand with Ross Bertram, I was disappointed with the length of time it took to develop the proper technique. Ross spent the first two years deprogramming the bad habits and inappropriate thinking that impeded my work, habits that I had acquired by collecting information on an ad hoc basis that I was only too eager to apply. I did not take the time to analyze the proper technique and its application. I just wanted to rush ahead and start to perform. I quickly discovered that with expert guidance anyone can learn these principles. It just takes commitment and effort.

The great inventor Thomas Edison attributed his own success to hard work rather than divine inspiration. His formula for success was 10 percent inspiration and 90 percent perspiration. For many years I took issue with Edison's equation. There had to be an easier way to achieve success. Who wants to perspire 90 percent of the time? There must be, in the parlance of the legal profession, a loophole. I was quite proud of myself when I discovered the solution. Success could be redefined as 10 percent inspiration, 10 percent perspiration and 80 percent preparation. My experience as a performer and as a tax lawyer had taught me that I did not perspire nearly as much if I was prepared. Unfortunately my redefinition was not to last very long when one of my clients pointed out that 99 percent of preparation is, in fact, perspiration!

So was Edison right after all: success is 10 percent inspiration and 90 percent perspiration? There are no short cuts. Success comes to those who work really hard. Anyone who appears to be successful and promulgates the idea that success came without effort is lying. He or she is trying to create the impression—the illusion—of success without work because that is the secret wish of most members of society: fame and fortune without work. There is a lesson to be learned however. The lesson is that we have to decide where and when we are willing to perspire. We can perspire on our own terrain or on someone else's. I prefer my own domain. Not only does it create the illusion that results appear without effort and that my natural abilities—or magic powers—are out of the ordinary but it also reduces stress. Choosing where and when to perspire is part of learning how to manage the process. It is also just one decision of many that have to be made to solve a particular problem.

Professional cardsharps have to make many decisions. They can play by "the rules" or by their own rules. If they play by the latter—Advantage Play—they will incur more risk but also increase their opportunity for profit. How and when and on what basis the executive or manager elects to make that decision is all part of the process. CEOs and entrepreneurs agree, it must be an informed decision, not a foolish or impulsive one.

Now what is the art of creative problem solving? Art is about choice. The artist must decide the subject for his art and the medium in which he can express it. In a painting, the artist must determine the composition in the frame and choose which colors he must draw from his pallet. The artist must make decisions about the type of brush to use and the style of brushstrokes to paint. It is the same in every artistic endeavor. Each work is really the product of hundreds of tiny decisions, which taken individually appear to be insignificant but when grouped as a whole produce an artistic triumph.

In the corporate arena, we make the same decisions

as the artist. Business—like art—is about choice. We must make decisions—thoughtful decisions. Whether your executive mandate is increasing sales, deciding how to organize your company's agenda and priorities, or deciding how to allocate resources in an advertising campaign, you have the opportunity to exercise thought in the same manner as any other artist. The mechanics of problem solving provide a framework for making the right decisions. You will feel more empowered if you take stock of the decisions that you are required to make.

Compare the number of decisions you make every day by rote to the decisions you actually plan for, think about, and enact. Most are immediate, off-the-cuff, intuitive. There should always be more opportunity for thoughtful decision making and with that more efficient problem solving.

Life becomes much more interesting when you accept the fact that you constantly make decisions and that each decision has consequences or ramifications that trickle down. Countless management studies and workplace surveys indicate that many people do not find their jobs to be very engaging, rewarding, or stimulating. Yet beneath the surface of even the most mundane activities lies the opportunity for creative problem solving and, like lifting a rock in a garden and discovering tiny mysterious creatures squirming beneath, vitality and potential for growth exists everywhere if we are willing to look for it. Even the most ordinary endeavor is teeming with the opportunity to benefit from well-founded, well-grounded decisions. Where there is choice, there is opportunity for success—frequently between a rock and a hard place. So, in business we find ourselves in the same position as the cardsharp and the artist. We have to make decisions.

In offering this work I will try to avoid the word "creativity" as much as possible. I am not so much interested in the *creative* as I am in delivering *effective* solutions. I am a pragmatist when it comes to business. People who deliver effective solutions are often labeled creative. On a primary level, exercising creativity means making informed decisions. But the ability to solve problems that withstand the tests of time and counter-active competition becomes even more important in an ever-changing world. If the Zen philosophical statement that "change is the only constant in life" is correct, the solutions developed for problems of today might not apply tomorrow. People who fear change do so because they do not understand Advantage Play and the mechanics of problem solving. They can only apply cookie cutter solutions and hope that they work. The result is fear and anxiety. It is not their fault; they have not been taught the mechanics of Advantage Play in problem solving. Professional problem solvers regard change as an opportunity to profit from exercising their creativity. S. W. Erdnase wrote "There is but one pleasure in life greater than winning, that is, in making the hazard."

Consider these caveats. First, there are no simple magical, sleight-of-hand solutions. Miracles happen one step at a time. This is the real secret to magic. It is misleading to think that any result—be it in a magician's performance or business problem solving—can be attributed to a single cause. That is like saying the magician creates a miracle by using mirrors or by having everything pass up or down the sleeve. These simplistic inferences deliver nothing in the real world of business. Success is based on the cumulative effect of a series of studied, apparently inconsequential details.

Second, I am not going to tell you how to manage your business. When I speak to corporations about problem solving, I never tell them how to run their businesses; I tell them how I run mine. The parallels are sufficiently clear that people walk away with new insights into how to manage their affairs and become better problem solvers. I have taken the same approach in this book. You will learn much about my business. It will be up to you, however, to apply the principles of Advantage Play and creative problem solving to your own business or profession.

Finally, although this book is about creative problem solving, I have included several magic tricks as illustrations. But this is not a book about learning magic to incorporate into a business presentation to win friends and influence people or deceive colleagues. I will not denigrate my profession by telling you that it is easy to perform magic tricks. Books that claim to teach magic to the public are so sophomoric that the author, performer, and audience should be embarrassed. Magicians spend countless hours learning how to perform. It is foolhardy to perform without training. You wouldn't do it in your profession. I don't do it in mine.

A D V A N T A G E   P L A Y

1. Success is 10 percent inspiration, 10 percent perspiration and 80 percent preparation.
2. You have control over where and when you perspire.
3. People who deliver effective solutions are often labeled creative.
4. Change is an opportunity to profit from exercising creativity.
5. The opportunity for thoughtful decision-making is often between a rock and a hard place.
6. Every magical effect is the product of a series of seemingly inconsequential details.
7. Anyone who appears to be successful and who states that his or her success came without effort is lying.

CHAPTER TWO

The Mechanics of Problem Solving

Hence it will be seen that proficiency in one
artifice does not finish the education of the
professional card player, and almost every
ruse in the game is more or less dependent
upon another one.

S. W. ERDNASE

MANY OF MY CORPORATE CLIENTS believe that the jump from law into magic and management consulting was a huge leap. Perhaps it was a matter of economics. But intellectually, creatively, I believe there was virtually no change. I am now just working in a different medium. Over the years I had developed an extensive Rolodex of acquaintances from a variety of corporate cultures: lawyers, magicians, developers, psychics, and stock promoters. I enjoyed the time I spent with all of them. They were full of life and energy and had minds that seemed to tower over others. They seemed—for lack of a better word—to be creative people always generating new ideas, schemes, and approaches from which they derived their livelihood. Most of all, they seemed to enjoy what they did and they enjoyed it despite the challenges they faced on a day-to-day basis. I realized we had a lot in common.

So, what do cardsharps, magicians, and business

executives have in common? People expect them to perform the impossible. The cardsharp is expected to laugh in the face of probability and orchestrate the winning hand. The illusionist is expected to defy the laws of nature and perform a magical effect. The tax lawyer is expected to make one of life's two certainties—death and taxes—disappear. Business executives too must strike the word "impossible" from their vocabularies to achieve success. Now, the impossible is really nothing more than a problem waiting to be solved. As a group, all these individuals are professional problem solvers.

Capitalist economies are based on the reward system. Do something well—solve a problem—reap the reward. People get paid to solve problems and you can define payment in any manner you desire. Payment can be a monetary reward or the personal satisfaction for completing a job well done. Both vocational and avocational enterprises are measured by this yardstick.

For most people, confronting a problem is their worst fear. They have not been taught a discipline to solve problems. They assume that education, training, and work experience have equipped them with the requisite skills, each individual developing his or her own methodology for problem solving in an ad hoc manner by absorbing various techniques through osmosis from their educational or business environment. This is not a very effective or efficient way to learn the most essential life skill.

Professional problem solvers understand that creating solutions is a mechanical exercise. Like hitting a golf or tennis ball, the proper mechanics will take you far. When faced with a problem, Advantage Play executives do not wait for divine inspiration to provide them with the solution. They understand that technique—properly applied—allows them to create solutions on demand.

The problem-solving process can be broken down mechanically into four steps. The first step is to define the objective. The second is to define the options for solutions. The third step is to evaluate the options. The fourth is to implement the best possible solution. Now, you may be thinking this analysis is simplistic and naive. I am not offended. Before you dismiss the analysis, answer this question: what is the next logical number in the following sequence?

$$18 \quad 00 \quad 26 \quad 54 \quad 87 \quad ?$$

The answer happens to be 0. Did you get it? No? The answer is 0 because 0 is that last digit in the phone number of my agent. He can be reached at 1-800-265-4870. As you can see the numeric sequence 18 00 26 54 87 0 is his phone number. I don't have to be psychic to know what you are thinking. You're thinking: there is no way I could have gotten that number! I don't even know who your agent is, let alone know his phone number! It doesn't matter.

Try it out on a friend. Write your friend's phone number out in the manner set forth above, that is break it up into two digit intervals and leave the last digit blank. Then ask the friend to tell you what the next logical number is in the sequence. Put on some additional pressure by saying that she should know it! As soon as she signals defeat, fill in the sequence with the missing digit. Amazingly, even then your friend may not see it until you regroup the numbers in their familiar pattern. Explain that she should have known the number as it happens to be her phone number. Re-write the sequence if you need to so that your friend understands. She will react much the way that you did.

So, what does this tell us? It teaches us several things. First, it illustrates the old adage: "The obscure we see eventually, the obvious takes a lot longer." In hind-sight it is obvious that the sequence of numbers represents a phone number. We complicate our lives, however, by looking for obscure solutions when the obvious ones will do. Sometimes we work so hard to find an obscure permutation or insight into a problem that we overlook the obvious solution. Our perceptions inhibit our ability to recognize the obvious. Be honest. One of the reasons you were fooled in the first place is that your mind was searching for a complicated solu-tion—an obscure solution—so much so that it missed the obvious.

Second, the phone number puzzle illustrates that sometimes it does not matter how hard we work, we will never develop the solution because we are not approaching the task of solving the problem in the right manner. Time management—or the lack thereof—remains a perennial problem in business. If you took an inventory of people with whom you work and outlined each person's approach to time management, most likely you will discover co-workers or colleagues who work very hard and devote tremendous amounts of time to their labors but some of them will achieve more suc-cess than others. Conventional wisdom states that rewards come to those who work hard. Sometimes, however, this is simply not true. Dai Vernon learned at an early age that a sleight would have no effect unless he knew how to *get into it* and *get out of it* without being detected. He had to understand *the approach*. Advantage Players focus on their approach to solving problems as much as they do on developing the options that can make the problem disappear.

The Mechanics of Problem Solving is a common sense approach to problem solving. The approach is universal. The business executive uses the same four-step procedure to make obstacles disappear as the magician does to perform the impossible. Don't be disappointed if the approach seems so simple. Most people who discover the secret behind a magic trick are disappointed with the simplicity of the modus operandi. The modus operandi only appears to be simple because it has been subjected to decades of professional judgment. Magicians from all around the world have studied, tested, debated, and developed the most economical and efficient manner in which to achieve the effect. It is the same with The Mechanics of Problem Solving.

Also, do not assume that just because something appears to be common sense that it is easy to apply. Simple ideas are deceptive ideas, deceptive in that they require attention to detail to be delivered effectively and efficiently. Attack each problem in a measured manner—one step at a time—and the problem will disappear. Let me teach you a magic trick that illustrates this principle. You will learn how to perform an impossible feat, that is to predict the outcome of a future event. First, let me describe the words and images that create *the effect*.

SLEEP ON IT

"*M* *ost people have experienced some form of psychic impression, call it déjà vu. The difference between most people and myself is that I write my predictions down. As a case in point, I had an impression last night about an event. I believe that the event is unfolding as we speak. There is only one way to test it. Shuffle this deck of cards.*" The spectator shuffles the deck and then hands it back to the performer. The performer asks, "*Would you like to shuffle the cards some more or are you satisfied that they are truly mixed?*" The spectator is satisfied with the condition of the cards.

The performer continues, "*Here is my prediction: 18, 24, 42, 5, 17, 33 … I'm sorry, wrong dream. Those are the winning numbers in next week's lottery. Ah, here we are.*" The performer removes a small billet from his wallet. "*I will deposit my thoughts about this event in this wine glass prior to the unfolding of the event. Here we go.*

"*My dream was very simple. I imagined that someone, well to be quite honest—you—cut a deck of cards. Don't ask me why. It was, after all, a dream. So, humor me. Please cut the cards.*" The spectator cuts the cards. "*We will mark the cut. Well, the next thing that happened was, well, I woke up! I know—not so exciting. I told you it was a simple dream. At least I remembered it. Well, as soon as I woke up I wrote down the name of the playing card that first popped into my head. Wouldn't it be strange if the card that you cut to matched the identity of the card that I imagined you cut to after waking up from my dream? I'd say so, particularly since you shuffled and cut the deck yourself. Go ahead, open up the paper and see what I wrote."* The spectator opens the billet and sees the name of a playing card. *"Let's take a look at the card that you cut to."* The spectator turns over the cut card. A perfect match! *"Would you like to see that again? Unfortunately I have to sleep on it!"*

Unfortunately it is not possible to predict the future with any consistent degree of accuracy. It is possible, however, to create that impression if you do so one step at a time. The real secret of being able to predict the future is to control the event after the prediction has been made so that the outcome matches the prediction. In *Sleep on It*, first you make a prediction and then you make the spectator select the predicted card. Magicians call this *forcing* a card. I call it *Virtual Participation*.

To perform this trick you require a deck of cards, a pen, several pieces of paper, and a wine glass. Prepare several predictions about different events on slips of paper. Record the name of the card that you are going to force on one of these slips of paper. Place all of the papers in your wallet.

Hand a deck of cards to a spectator and ask him or her to shuffle the cards. Take the deck back from the spectator, spread the cards face up between your hands and ask him or her if he or she is satisfied that the cards have been mixed. As you spread the cards, note the position of the card you have predicted and separate your hands at that card so that the predicted card is the bottom card of the cards in the right hand. **(Photograph 1)** Once the spectator indicates he or she is satisfied, place the cards in the left hand on top of the cards in the right hand. **(Photograph 2)** Turn the deck face down and place it on the table. The predicted card—the card you will force the spectator to select—is on top of the deck.

Remove the slips of paper from your wallet and read a couple of them out loud. Eventually place the card prediction, unread, into a wine glass. Ask the spectator to cut the cards wherever she or he would like and table the packet. Pick up the bottom portion of the deck and place it perpendicular to and across the back of the top

portion. **(Photograph 3)** You are "marking the cut." Tell your little story about the prediction. Ask the spectator to open the slip of paper and read the prediction. When you say wouldn't it be a coincidence if the card the spectator cut to matched the name of the card that you wrote down as a result of your dream, pick up the top portion of the deck **(Photograph 4)**, deal off the top card of the bottom portion—the force card—to the table and replace the top portion back square on top of the deck. You have forced the prediction. To conclude the performance, dramatically turn the card over on the table revealing the correct match.

Now that you know the secret, go back and analyze each component of it. Make sure that you understand the objective so that you can communicate it effectively to your audience. Analyze the methodology to see how the many apparently inconsequential details orchestrate the effect. Finally, commit yourself to the entire process: establishing the premise with story and props, conducting the process of cutting to the force card, and concluding the piece in an effective and amusing manner. The trick will be effective only if you commit yourself to the entire process. It is the same in business. The Advantage Player, be it an organization or an individual, must commit to the entire process; that is, each stage of the problem-solving sequence. Half measures are never sufficient.

If you survey the literature on creativity and business, most of the texts provide excellent suggestions on how to generate ideas. Few, however, place idea generation techniques in the context of the process of problem solving. Ideas are worthwhile if they achieve an objective, are properly evaluated, and effectively implemented. The law of intellectual property—copyright, trademarks, and patents—provides an excellent example. Another old adage states, "Ideas are not subject to copyright because supply exceeds demand." Good intentions are not worth much in the marketplace because everyone has them. Under copyright law, for example, you could tell your life story to someone who could write it down word for word and yet you would receive no copyright interest in the work. It is the person who picked up the pen and wrote it down who gets the protection. Similarly, you receive trademark protection by either using the mark in the marketplace or by filing the appropriate forms with the government agency. Finally, it is not the inventor who first comes up with the idea for an invention who obtains patent protection; it is the person who is first to file the appropriate forms—the patent claim and specification—who obtains the protection.

Innovative companies now eschew the notion that creative ideas are developed first for their own sake, independent of any particular application, and then stockpiled for some future use. They realize that the ability to generate ideas is of little use unless it is part of a managed strategy for success. Creative ideas must be directed toward a concrete objective—solving a client's problem—and then evaluated and implemented to have value in the marketplace. Professional problem solvers adopt a step-by-step approach. They are committed to the entire process of problem solving and not just the aspect that deals with generating ideas.

Fortunately, you do not have to spend thousands of

dollars to try to improve your problem-solving skills. You do not have to videotape the mechanics of your approach to problem solving as you would a tennis stroke, golf swing, or bottom deal. You can review your approach to problem solving each and every day at little or no cost. When you face a difficult problem, review exactly where you are in the process. Have you defined the objective? Have you reviewed all options? Have you determined the best solutions? Have you implemented the best solution properly? Just like a professional athlete who goes off her game, the Advantage Play executive will isolate her company's deficiencies and take corrective measures. When you have a difficult time solving a problem, examine the mechanics of your thought process to make sure that everything is proceeding according to plan. The solution may be something as simple as renewing your commitment to each step of the process.

Finally, the executive who is an Advantage Player will always try to reduce the role that chance plays in any transaction. By taking charge, planning, and then executing the plan one step at a time, the Advantage Player can make the miracle happen. As S. W. Erdnase stated so simply at the beginning of this chapter, "Almost every ruse in the game is more or less dependent upon another one."

A D V A N T A G E   P L A Y

1. Success comes to those who solve problems.
2. Solving problems is a mechanical exercise.
3. Technique properly applied allows you to solve problems on demand.
4. Every problem can be solved in four steps: define the objective, generate solutions, evaluate the solutions, and implement the solution.
5. Don't complicate your life by looking for obscure solutions when obvious ones will do.
6. Simple solutions are deceptive in that they require enormous attention to detail to work properly.
7. Commit to the entire process and not just one particular aspect of it.
8. Eliminate chance by taking charge, planning, and then executing the plan one step at a time.

CHAPTER THREE

The Real Work

The finished card expert considers nothing
too trivial that in any way contributes to his
success, whether in avoiding or allaying sus-
picion, or in the particular manner of
carrying out each detail; or in leading up to,
or executing each artifice.

S. W. ERDNASE

I MAGINE YOU ARE A FAMOUS MAGICIAN performing in the Mecca of Magic—London, England—in 1902. You wake up one morning, pour yourself a cup of tea, and open *The Times*. You turn to the entertainment section. A headline grabs your attention. "Magician makes woman float in mid-air." You can't believe what you are reading. A woman floating in mid-air! Impossible. It can't be done. You read further. It's true. Your competitor has become the first magician to make a person float above the stage without any apparent physical means of support. You close your eyes and contemplate the unimaginable. You realize that if you do not create this same illusion on stage, your audience will abandon you. They will flock to see the magician who can make someone float. The only thing you know for sure is that your competitor is not going to tell you how it is done. You must figure it out on your own.

Fast forward to the year 2001. You have left your current place of employment to set up your own e-commerce business. As a well-configured enterprise, you can conduct business from just about anywhere, but you are not sure how you should structure the organization. Should it be a sole proprietorship or an incorporated entity? Where should the principal place of business be? Which countries or jurisdictions will subject you to taxes? How do you determine the best course of action?

Whether you are forced to make "The Woman Float in Mid-Air" or face a unique business opportunity, approach both tasks in the same manner. Apply The Mechanics of Problem Solving and the solution will materialize. To do this, however, you must understand *The Real Work*. The Real Work is a term used by Advantage Players to describe the most refined and sophisticated techniques that convert a good trick into a miracle or a secret sleight into something that "gets the money." The search for The Real Work is a lifetime pursuit in which no piece of information is considered too trivial. We will now examine each stage of The Mechanics of Problem Solving to unearth The Real Work.

Step One: Define the Objective

Magicians define the objective as *the effect*. The starting point for all magic is the effect. Magicians do not care how the effect is achieved. The effect can be defined as each audience member's recollection of what took place. Perception is reality. Unless *the effect* is properly constructed, each audience member may form a different impression of what took place. This dilutes the impact of the performance. The audience must understand in unequivocal terms the nature of *the effect*. If audience members cannot comprehend what has taken place, they will not react appropriately. Even worse, they will not be able to explain what has happened to other people. The biggest mistake a magician can make is to assume the audience understands what took place. The *effect* must always be presented clearly.

This same principle applies in business and is particularly relevant where teams have been assembled to solve problems since errors are often compounded exponentially in group situations. Everyone may *think* that they know what the objective is when, in fact, few are in actual agreement. Your own experiences may illustrate this. Examine the recent problems you have encountered that were particularly time consuming. Was a large amount of the inefficiency due to the fact that the objective was poorly articulated or even changed part way through the process? Did a client or colleague say, "What I really meant to say was this" or "This is not exactly what I wanted"? Advantage Players would call these *tells*—inconsistencies in action that tip off the deception. A magician would say that such actions *telegraph* the technique and dilute the impact of *the effect*. Such *tells* must be eliminated.

Methodology is secondary. Magicians will revert to practically anything in order to achieve the desired *effect*. Every problem deserves a customized solution. It is rare that a ready-made solution can come off the shelf and solve the problem. Every problem regardless of how familiar it may appear has its nuances. Often people believe they know the client's business so well they assume they know what the client is asking for. As a result, the client's objectives are not really heard. We fail to see that the needs of the client have changed. Needs change on a daily basis. It is not your client's fault. It is your fault because you did not take the time to understand the problem and define the objective. You made the assumption that you knew the objective. When a client states, "What I really meant to say was this," he or she is really saying, "Since you didn't get my objective the first time, I'll try to rephrase it in this manner."

The solution: listen to the client and resist the temptation to look like a hero by rushing in and delivering a random solution. This is more difficult to do than it sounds. We often propose a solution just because we want to appear as if we are working hard. Resist the temptation to look busy. We do this because our society emphasizes conspicuous activity instead of intellectual activity: make that call, order that supply, confirm that delivery time, practice that bottom deal. Your own experience should confirm this. If you work in a corporate environment, walk past an open door and you may see a colleague staring into space. You probably assume the person in that office is daydreaming about his or her favorite sports team, family vacation, or luncheon date. You might accuse your colleague of thinking of everything but the task at hand. Yet perhaps your colleague is, in fact, *using his head*, thinking about the problem at hand.

There are many factors that force us to jump in without having thought sufficiently about the problem we are trying to solve. Domestic pressure, demands from colleagues, sales quotas, year-ends, market fluctuations, pending mergers all exact their toll. We will never be able to extricate ourselves from all of them. We do, however, have to develop the discipline and techniques to manage these demands. Recognize that pressures exist and place them in perspective. By doing so you will save time in the end. It is more efficient to deliver the correct solution the first time rather than return again and again to the drawing board after delivering a half-baked idea or an ill-fitting garment all in the name of expediency. You have to *use your head*.

Part of becoming an Advantage Player is learning to be a good listener and asking the right questions. In the corporate environment, lawyers know that clients rarely articulate their actual objective. A client is aware that he or she might have a problem but is not aware of the extent of the problem or how to describe it. It is the lawyer's task to help to determine the nature of the problem that forms the basis for the client's objective. Failure to do so could prove catastrophic. The objective will only materialize when the lawyer reveals it by questioning. Just as the lawyer must ask questions and flag everything that can go wrong with a transaction before advising the client how to deal with the problem, Advantage Players know that it is their responsibility to make sure the objective is properly understood before embarking on the process of generating solutions. Fortunately there are techniques of Advantage Play you can use to help define each objective.

Define the problem—the objective—in unambiguous terms. Objective: Make the woman float in mid-air. What could be clearer? This focus will save time, energy, and money. Dai Vernon stated that for *an effect* to be *effective*, the audience must be able to describe the effect in one simple sentence. Not only will the audience members then understand exactly what took place but they will also be able to tell other people what happened. This is how legends are created. Nothing illustrates this better than the effect Dai Vernon used to fool Harry Houdini.

It was on February 6, 1922, at the Great Northern Hotel in Chicago at a banquet given by local magicians in honor of Houdini after his evening performance at the theater. Vernon was twenty-eight, Houdini was fifty-two. Vernon asked Houdini to select a card from the pack. Vernon then asked Houdini to write his initials onto the face of the card. Houdini wrote H.H. The card was returned face down to the top of the pack. With one hand Vernon openly shifted Houdini's card from the top to the second position, that is beneath the first card of the pack. Vernon made a magical gesture and then turned over the top card. It was now the card that Houdini had signed. Houdini asked Vernon to repeat the effect. Vernon complied and once again the initialed card rose to the top. Houdini was perplexed. The effect was simple and straightforward. There could be no duplicate cards involved because he himself had initialed the card. Houdini asked Vernon to repeat the effect a third time. Once again Vernon did the trick slowly and deliberately. Again, the card rose to the top. Vernon repeated the effect eight times in total. Houdini had no idea how it was performed and later was forced to admit that he—Harry Houdini—had been fooled by this young man. Shortly afterwards, Dai Vernon was being promoted in New York City as "The Man Who Fooled Houdini."

Now, Vernon could have performed almost anything

and he would have fooled Houdini. He chose a simple *effect*, an *effect* that could be described in one simple sentence: a signed card rose to the top of the pack. By performing something that could be described in one simple sentence, each audience member understood not only exactly what took place but also was able to go away and tell other people what happened. Vernon knew that simple was more effective.

David Copperfield—ranked number three behind Houdini and Vernon in *Magic Magazine*'s best of the century poll—adheres to this principle. Copperfield always closes his network television specials with a startling illusion. He has walked through the Great Wall of China and made the Statue of Liberty and a Learjet vanish—each of which as an effect can be described in a simple sentence.

You may be saying to yourself that it may be easy to break magical effects into simple one-sentence tasks but your business is much more sophisticated than performing a magic trick. I disagree. It is just as important in business to break the objective down into a series of simple one-sentence tasks as it is in magic. If you cannot describe each objective in one simple sentence, there will be a breakdown in communication somewhere along the chain and you will not be able to perform or deliver an efficient solution. The bottom line is that regardless of how large you perceive the problem to be, if you break it up into individual, simple one-sentence tasks and you attack them one by one, the problem will disappear. You have to *use your head*. There is no such thing as magic. You cannot wave a wand or chant some incantation to make the problem disappear.

Of course, this takes effort. Many people break objectives into smaller units intuitively. Dai Vernon preferred a more disciplined approach because although intuition can be useful, it often leaves gaps. The gaps are created because we fool ourselves into believing that we have intuitive responses to problems, when in fact we just do not want to put in the requisite amount of work to define the objective or deliver the solution.

Second, Advantage Players separate *the effect* from *the method* and, in particular, do not let the methodology dictate the effect. Emotions often run high in business and there is always the danger of allowing a motivation, a product, or a procedure to determine the course of events despite the fact that the motivation, product, or procedure does not accomplish the objective. One of the cardinal rules in business is to avoid structuring transactions purely on the basis of the tax ramifications. Tax ramifications are important but they are not the sole criterion on which transactions should be based. Tax professionals caution clients to avoid having the tail wag the dog, so to speak. Many tax shelters, however, are structured precisely in this manner. They encourage people to invest in speculative ventures on the basis that most investors would prefer to lose money in a high-risk venture than pay the government taxes.

Once you separate *the effect* from *the method*, realizing that each requires its own style of thinking, one linear and the other non-linear, anything becomes possible. Again, the illusion of a person floating in the air is a suitable case study. Although *the effect* of levitation has become a staple in the modern magician's repertoire, only once—and it was televised—have I witnessed the subject float from the stage, hover above the heads of the audience, and then return to the stage. Although it was performed on television, it was performed without the aid of camera trickery. The secret demonstrates the importance of understanding *the effect* and separating it conceptually from *the methodology.*

The solution was simple in concept. The assistant who was suspended in mid-air did not move one inch. Instead, the magician shifted the entire studio audience forward, beneath the floating assistant. It was a lateral solution—literally and figuratively. It appeared on television, however, that the woman floated above the heads of the audience. The audience was then secretly shifted back to its original position to create the illusion that the assistant floated back above their heads. Perception is reality.

Although this trick was obvious to the studio audience—in retrospect one can see how the viewer at home could mistake the studio audience's collective gasp of amazement a nanosecond *before* the floating lady traversed the airwaves as a gasp of amazement at the apparent levitation—the magician's objective was to make it appear to the millions of viewers who were watching on television that the person floated above the heads of the audience. The magician did not care that a studio audience of one hundred people were not only let in on the secret but also manipulated like an inanimate object in order to create the illusion for his real audience—the television audience. All he cared about was achieving his objective.

Step Two: Generate Solutions

Once you have determined the objective or more correctly the objectives or effects that you want to achieve,
it is time to figure out how to fulfill those objectives. You
have to generate solutions. You are in the second stage
of The Mechanics of Problem Solving.

So how does one generate such brilliant solutions,
and in the case of the televised levitation, lateral solutions? Again, the answer is simple to describe but
difficult to implement. You must learn to suspend your
logical reasoning skills and challenge all assumptions. A
primary reason a business will fail to generate an effective solution is that the business relies too much on
logical reasoning and, in particular, erroneous assumptions. This is our default mode of thinking. We have
been conditioned to think in logical terms from an early
age. Advantage Players, however, turn the negative into
a positive. Magicians fool people, for example, by taking
stock of the assumptions that each audience member
brings to the performance and then capitalizes on these
assumptions. If the audience sees the magician place a
bottle of Coke™ into a paper bag and the bag is crum-
pled into a small ball, the audience will assume that the
bottle has vanished. The audience makes this assumption because it assumes that the bottle is made of glass
and contains carbonated soda. The audience makes the
assumption that the Coke™ bottle is real because it looks
so real. Unbeknownst to the audience, however, the
Coke™ bottle is actually made of latex rubber and can be
compressed easily into a small space.

The first step to generate solutions is to recognize

and identify the assumptions one makes. This is harder than it sounds. It is not enough to know that you have to challenge assumptions, you must actively take the steps to mentally and physically do so if you want to discover The Real Work, a great creative solution. Most people give up thinking too soon.

Let me illustrate this with a simple brainteaser.

$$92 - 63 = 1$$

How do you move one digit in such a fashion that the equation becomes true? Spend at least a few moments on it before you give up. Most people try to solve the puzzle by inverting the number 9 so that it becomes a 6. Unfortunately this does not produce the answer. 62 – 63 does not equal 1! This problem requires a lateral solution—again literally and figuratively. The solution *is* to invert the number 9 *but* move it so that it becomes an exponential number: $2^6 - 63 = 1$.

If you had difficulty solving this problem—and most people do—it is because you made an assumption rather than challenged one. You assumed that the equation had to be solved on the same linear plane on which it was written. The only thing this assumption guaranteed was failure. The concept of the non-linear (literally and figuratively) exponential number never entered the equation, so to speak. More important, it would not make any difference how hard you worked on the problem. If you make an erroneous assumption about the strategic approach to developing the solution, you could work on this problem for days and not see the solution.

Here is another example. Imagine there are 3 cups

of coffee and 36 cubes of sugar in front of you. How do you distribute the 36 cubes of sugar among the 3 cups of coffee so that you end up with an odd amount in each cup? The answer is to place 1 cube in the first cup, 1 cube in the second cup and 34 cubes of sugar in the third cup, which—you have to admit—is an *odd* amount of sugar in a cup of coffee!

Most have difficulty solving this puzzle because they assume that it is the same type of puzzle as the previous one. That is, the solution is based on mathematical notation. This is not surprising as I intentionally placed the $92 - 63 = 1$ brainteaser in advance of this one to manipulate your mode of thinking. The solution has nothing to do with mathematics. It has everything to do with language and the interpretation of the word "odd". Again, once you blindly commit to a particular definition—and our society is plagued with definitions—much of your work may be in vain. Every problem is unique. Just ask your customers. It certainly is from their perspective. It is dangerous to make the assumption that a subsequent transaction can be treated in the same manner as an earlier transaction or that one problem can be solved in exactly the same manner as an earlier problem. Assumptions must be challenged on an on-going basis. If the only thing constant in life is change, the assumptions that you make today may not apply tomorrow. This is a critical point.

One simple but excellent technique for challenging assumptions is to set a minimum quota of ideas that must be generated before moving on to the next stage of the problem-solving sequence. Advantage Players are never satisfied with the first solution that presents itself.

Take, for example, the famous nine-dot puzzle associated with Edward de Bono in which the participant is requested to draw four straight connected lines so that they pass through each dot only once.

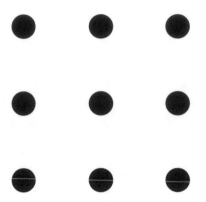

The solution, which has become a visual metaphor for lateral thinking and shifting your paradigm, depends on the participant extending a line outside the box. Hence the term *thinking outside the box.*

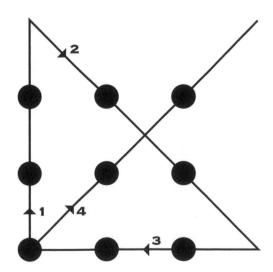

It is also possible to complete a similar task, that is to pass a line through all nine dots with just one line, in at least three different ways. One way is to place the piece of paper with the matrix of nine dots against the side of a sphere like a globe, place a pencil on the top dot and slowly spin the globe around as you work the pencil ever downward in one cylindrical line that eventually passes through each dot. A second way is to fold the paper in such a manner so that each dot overlaps the other and then thrust the point of the pencil through it passing the line of the pencil *through* each dot. A third way is to change the size of the writing instrument and make a line so wide that one stroke is sufficient to pass through each dot simultaneously. This third solution, in particular—changing the size of the line so that one line passes through all nine dots—should remind the reader that innovative solutions are often derived from something as simple as challenging a definition. Most definitions are imposed by legislation or convenience and once established rarely change, despite the fact that everything else in the world has changed around them. The Advantage Player is unlikely to discover these various options unless he or she sets the goal of generating three or four or five possible solutions and is willing to flag and challenge each definition encountered along the way.

Let me give you an example from the world of business. In this case, it is the business of cardsharping. As you would expect, using marked cards—cards that have been secretly marked in a manner known only to the cardsharp—provides a distinct advantage. As gamblers have become more aware of marking systems, cardsharps have been forced to adapt and improve such systems in order to maintain their competitive advantage at the table. A quick survey of such techniques will illustrate how inventive people develop solutions by challenging assumptions.

It used to be sufficient to secretly place an ink blot or other mark in a strategic location on the back of a card to differentiate one card from another. A seasoned gambler, however, may detect such a ruse simply by holding one end of the cards and riffling the other end, causing the cards to cascade off the fingertips like a child flicking individual cells of an animated picture book. If the cards are marked with ink blots, the markings will dart across the backs of cards during this riffling procedure. In gambling parlance, this procedural check is called "going to the movies."

A more sophisticated approach to marking cards— one that permits the deck to be examined without any telltale sign of marking—was developed to counter "going to the movies." The cards are still marked, of course, but the markings have been made in broad strokes on the back of each card with a chemical that remains invisible to the untrained eye. Called a "juice deck" because of the formula used in marking the cards, the markings only become visible when the cardsharp "racks his focus," that is blurs his vision. A player who focuses on the back design of the card will not see the marks; a player who blurs his vision will. Everything comes with a cost. For the "juice deck" the cost or weakness is that the cardsharp must supply or "ring in" the doctored deck, known in the trade as a "cold deck" or "cooler," without being caught.

This problem can be circumvented by the use of another marking system: "punch work." A deck with punch work is a deck with strategically placed Braille-like markings created by a needle pushing against the surface of the card to create a pinprick impression on each pertinent card. This impression can then be recognized by touch rather than by sight. A punch can take many forms. In one form, it is half a ball bearing with a needle sticking out. The flat base of the punch is made to adhere to the tip of the thumb. The cardsharp picks up the cards, which have been provided by the host, and proceeds to count them one at a time to the table ostensibly to make sure that the deck is complete. Every time the cardsharp comes across a card that may be useful during the game, that is, a high value card, he applies some additional pressure to the card with his fingers as he is dealing the card to the table so that the punch makes a small Braille-like mark in the card. The cardsharp can feel the identity of the card marked in this manner during the dealing procedure and elect where and when the card is ultimately dealt. It would be useful, of course, to have the marking system applied to both ends of the deck because one never knows how the cards will be mixed. To facilitate this the cardsharp will declare after he or she has counted the cards—and placed the punch work in one end of the deck—that the deck consists of only 51 cards. He or she will count them again—after turning them end for end—to double check the total. By counting the cards a second time the cardsharp secretly places the marking system in the other end of the deck.

Legend has it that one of the most elaborate marking

ploys was accomplished by a cardsharp who purchased a playing card manufacturing plant and secretly embedded his own secret marking system in the plates that printed the back design on the playing cards. This enterprising individual then undercut the price of supplying playing cards to casinos so that casinos would stock his factory made marked cards. The entrepreneur was then free to travel from casino to casino playing with the advantage of marked cards.

As you can see, there are many ways to achieve the objective. Advantage Players in business recognize that idea generation requires a different mode of thinking, one that recognizes and then challenges assumptions. The next chapter will outline in great detail a variety of techniques Advantage Players employ to generate a greater quantity of ideas. For now, let us explore The Real Work in the next step in The Mechanics of Problem Solving.

Step Three: Evaluate the Solutions

Once the objective has been defined and multiple options have been generated—the purpose of which is to provide more options to choose from during the evaluation stage and to provide you with alternatives if the one you ultimately select does not work out as planned—you have entered the third stage of The Mechanics of Problem Solving. It is time to focus on the quality of the idea rather than the quantity of ideas. You must determine which option is the one most likely to achieve your objective. Your ability to evaluate the best course of action may become your most valuable—and highly compensated—asset as people with the best judgment ultimately receive the greatest rewards.

The most successful business decision makers are also the ones who can determine what will and will not work. Fortunately just as there are techniques you can use to help define your objective and generate solutions, there are also tricks you can employ to help evaluate the best course of action.

The first is to remember the KISS principle: Keep It Simple, Stupid! Unfortunately this axiom of business is often misinterpreted. The KISS principle does not mean that the easiest method is necessarily the best method. Conversely, the most direct method is not always the easiest. Dai Vernon, for example, not only drew a distinction between the effect and the methodology, he also drew a distinction between the simplicity of the concept and the complexity of its execution. He realized that often the simplest approach to an effect was the one that required a very sophisticated method.

In addition to *Erdnase*, Michelangelo inspired Dai Vernon. He often recited two maxims attributed to this great artist. Taken together they provide a dynamic range for evaluating ideas. At one end of the spectrum there is Michelangelo's comment: "Details make for perfection but perfection is no detail." At the other end of the spectrum is another observation: "Sometimes the means of expression can become so exquisite that the effect is lost."

The key is balance. But how does one recognize a balanced approach? The easiest way is to apply another truism from business: "Pigs get fat, hogs get slaughtered!" In the tax world, this rule tells you that while it may be okay to be piggish when you claim those deductions, you are not advised to be a hog because you will likely irritate a revenue authority who will order an investigation. Advantage Play executives suggest strategy but also evaluate the risk associated with each strategy. They must determine whether their clients are being pigs or hogs. To do this they apply the *smell test*. Does a client smell like a pig or smell like a hog?

So what is a sense of smell? A sense of smell is nothing more than a person taking stock of his inventory of experience and the inventory of experience of the people he works with to make an educated appraisal of the situation. Ultimately, people are really paid for their sense of smell. Anyone can ask the right questions to define the objective and anyone can generate solutions. The people who come to you to have their problems solved often don't care how you solve the problem as long as it is solved. They may pretend to be interested in how you arrived at your decision but in reality they could not care less. That is why they came to you in the first place. They rely on your sense of smell to tell them, "I have worked on transactions like this in the past. I recognize the fact that the only thing constant in life is change, and so I have taken into account variances from before. This is the way to go!" Ultimately this is how business is generated and relationships are formed. Your customers return to you because they trust your judgment. The most valuable asset of any organization is its people who can determine the best course of action for its clients.

Your business may employ a *Rainmaker*, a person who generates a significant amount of work or business for the enterprise. You may be one yourself. The term Rainmaker has a magical connotation. Often colleagues speak of Rainmakers in hushed tones, ever mindful of the mystique associated with the person who can drum up business through some shamanistic communication with a higher authority. In reality, the Rainmaker is someone with a well-developed and trusted sense of smell.

Part of developing a good sense of smell is developing a good Creative Infrastructure—a network that not only tracks past successes and failures but also encourages the exchange of information so that you, your colleagues, and your firm can harness that inventory of experience. When two corporations merge there is often a clash of corporate cultures. Instead of creating an atmosphere that promotes the exchange of ideas and the building of this inventory of experience, the participants adopt a siege mentality, each jockeying for position based on self-aggrandizing notions of merit and the quality of prescribed assumptions. Organizations have a greater chance of developing and implementing innovative solutions if they learn how to embrace and harness the diversity of the corporate cultures toward the common objective. We will explore how to build a *Creative Infrastructure* in the next chapter.

Finally, in the rare circumstance when two or more methods are equally effective, select the one that is the most original with you. This was the advice Dai Vernon received from his great friend, Charles Earl Miller— another superlative sleight-of-hand performer. Miller suggested that if all things are equal, pursue the solution that reflects your creativity, as you are more likely to invest the necessary energy to improve it further because it is your progeny.

With the objective defined, multiple options available, and the best option selected for the task, you are now ready for the final stage in The Mechanics of Problem Solving: implementation. If you do not implement the solution, everything will have been for naught. You will have wasted an incredible amount of time, energy, and money. It is not enough to come up with a good idea; you have to put it into practice.

Step Four: Implement The Solution

If you have nailed down the objective, challenged assumptions, generated good ideas, and determined the best course of action, it should be easy to implement the solution. You have finalized a plan. All you need now are the resources and the determination to see it through. Again, there are principles of Advantage Play that apply to both obtaining the necessary resources and guiding the project to completion.

The first requisite to obtaining the necessary resources is to sell the client on the merits of the solution. That's right. You have to sell the idea. I have always been astounded by the negative connotations associated with the word "sales". For many people the word "sales" is a dirty word. It seems that many organizations are separated into two divisions—a sales division and everyone else. Some people do not want to be placed in the sales category. I find this quite extraordinary. I believe that organizations are often crippled by this negative mindset. Creative problem solving is all about choice, and making decisions. When the decision-making process involves another person or entity—which it always does in business because business is all about solving problems—you have to persuade people that one choice is better than another. Thus, the concept of sales in and of itself is essential. The sale can be for the good in that it solves a problem—or it can be bad in the sense that the problem remains unsolved. I have never been interested in creating anything just for the sake of it. Even when I am experimenting—that is to say working without any commercial purpose in mind—I am doing it for a reason. The reason may be as simple as exploring a technique to see what other applications it may have. I want to see the effect that it may have on the problem that I am trying to solve. The only way to satisfy this desire is to sell people on the usefulness of the idea so that they embrace it as much as I do.

The first three steps in The Mechanics of Problem Solving also provide the framework for selling the value of your ideas to those who must *buy in* to them so that the solution can be implemented. Step One: confirm the objective. Step Two: brief the client on the assumptions that you challenged, the precedents on which you drew, and the solutions that you generated. Step Three: explain the evaluation process and what, in your opinion, it will take to get the solution implemented. You have to get a "yes" at each stage of the process. Three "yes" answers and you have sold them on your idea. This sales process does not have to take up a great deal of time. The sophistication of both the problem and the solution will dictate the length of time that is required to sell the idea.

Now, what if your solution does not solve the problem? After all, there are few guarantees. If you determined the appropriate objective, challenged assumptions and developed multiple solutions, evaluated them, and followed the strategy for implementation, it is not a mistake because anyone else would have done the same thing. It is only a mistake if you do not learn from the experience. Go back at it and try to deliver an alternative solution. If you followed The Mechanics of Problem Solving, you can use one of the other solutions that you developed during the idea-generation phase. If you have been monitoring the implementation, you will be able to alter the methodology. Remember, all you should be concerned with is *the effect*; it doesn't matter how you achieve it. Don't be afraid to switch the procedure during the implementation process if you can see that your best intention is not going to produce the desired result. The question you must ask continually is, "Are we achieving the objective?" Your customers or clients may not be concerned with the particular methodology. They just want to see the result. They want their problem solved.

If the problem persists it is time to go back to The Mechanics of Problem Solving and review each step of the process. If your golf swing, tennis stroke, or baseball swing is not producing results, you review it. The Advantage Play executive does the same thing. Review the mechanics of your problem-solving process to see what corrective measures need to be taken. Often this is the domain of consultants but I believe that everyone is capable of self-assessment if you are disciplined in your approach. The Mechanics of Problem Solving are much more sophisticated than meet the eye but once mastered enable the Advantage Play executive to solve problems in an innovative and effective manner.

It is time now to learn another magic trick. In this trick, you will predict the outcome of an event in advance—*without forcing the result.* The trick is called *Miraskill* and was created by Stewart James, someone Dai Vernon once described as one of the great minds in magic. First, I will storyboard *the effect* with words and images as I did with the previous trick so that you understand *the effect* from the point of view of the spectator. Remember that perception is reality. Second, I will explain *how* the trick works. Third, and most importantly for our purposes, I will explain *why* the trick works, our objective being to see how the trick illustrates the principles set out in this Chapter. Experience also tells me that you will enjoy performing the trick for family and friends.

MIRASKILL

"Have you ever heard of the game Rouge et Noir? No? Let me demonstrate." Performer hands the deck to the participant. *"Shuffle the cards as much as you would like. Make sure that neither you nor I have any idea of the order of the cards. In a moment I am going to have you turn the cards face up—two at a time. If they are both red cards, place them on one pile. If they are both black cards, place them on another pile. If, however, the pair consists of one red card and one*

*black card, consider them discards and place
them on a third pile.*

*"In Rouge et Noir, players would bet on the
turn of the cards. Some would bet that both cards
would be red, others black, and some both red
and black. I'm going to make my own bet in the
form of a prediction."* Performer writes something
on a piece of paper and places the prediction
face down on the table.

"Please, start turning over the pairs." The participant turns the cards over, two by two, and
places them in their respective piles. *"Now, count
the number of red cards in the red pile and then
count the number of cards in the black pile."* The
participant discovers that there are four more
black cards than red. *"Open my prediction. Even
though you shuffled the cards and did all the
dealing, my prediction was correct."* The performer's prediction does state that there will be
four more black cards than red.

*"Now, you may believe that I was just lucky. I
can assure you that luck has nothing to do with it.
Shuffle the cards again and I will make a new
prediction."* The performer drafts a new prediction and places it face down on the table. *"Now,
deal the cards as before."* Participant repeats the
dealing and sorting procedure. *"Once again,
please count the number of cards in the red pile
and compare it to the number of cards in the
black pile."* The participant discovers that the red
pile and the black pile each contain the same

number of cards. *"Oh, they are both the same? Here, look at my prediction."* The prediction is turned over and, once again, it is correct.

Now that you understand *the effect*, let me explain the principle of deception behind the effect. Stewart James discovered that if you take a deck of cards, shuffle them and then turn the cards face up two at a time and place them into the respective piles—red/red, black/black, and red/black—you will always have the same number of red cards in the red pile as you have black cards in the black pile regardless of how well the cards have been shuffled. Although the actual number of cards may differ each time, there will always be the same number of red cards as there will be black. If, however, you remove four cards of one color—say, red—from the pack and repeat the dealing procedure, you will end up with four more black cards than the red simply because the red cards have been removed from the equation. The objective is to transform this principle into a mystifying and entertaining *effect.*

To perform the sequence as discribed, secretly remove any four red cards from the pack prior to the performance. I suggest hiding them in an outside breast pocket. Start the performance by handing the pack to a spectator to shuffle the cards. Remove the pen and paper from your pocket and write your prediction: "You will have four more black cards than you will have red cards."

Explain the premise of the game of Rouge et

Noir and ask the spectator to deal the cards into
the respective piles. Every so often, however,
pick up the cards in the red/black pile from the
table—the discards—and place them in your outside breast pocket. At the conclusion of the
dealing procedure, ask the participant to count
the number of red cards and compare that number to the number of black. As he or she is
counting the respective piles, remove the cards
from your outside breast pocket (including the
four red cards you surreptitiously had concealed
there) and place them back on the table. Once
the spectator has finished counting, ask for the
number. He or she will state there are four more
black cards than red. Show them your prediction.

Offer to repeat the experiment. Push all the
cards toward the spectator to gather and shuffle
the cards. Write your new prediction: "You will
have the same number of black cards as you have
red." Ask the participant to deal the cards into the
respective piles: red/red, black/black, and
red/black. Once that task is completed, ask him
or her to count the respective number of cards in
the red and black piles. Each pile contains the
same number of cards. Show once again that you
have predicted the outcome.

Now that you know how *Miraskill* works, let's
explore *why* it works and draw from it principles that
can be applied in the business world. First, *Miraskill* is
a powerful *effect* because it can be described in a simple sentence. The performer predicts the outcome of a

future event. Second, the performer capitalizes on the spectator's acute logical reasoning skills and orchestrates the presentation to take advantage of the spectator's preconceptions. The spectator will assume, for example, that the deck consists of 52 cards; second, that the shuffling actually affects the potential outcome of the event; third, that the performer cannot manipulate the cards or the counting because the spectator is handling both; fourth, that the discards are meaningless; and fifth, that he or she is shuffling the same number of cards the second time as the first. All are erroneous assumptions. *Miraskill* is difficult to reconstruct because the spectator assumes that the second sequence mirrors the first except for the outcome of the prediction. The second phase, however, is to the first phase as 36 cubes of sugar into 3 cups of coffee is to $92 - 63 = 1$. The spectator who fails to recognize this will never reconstruct the method.

Finally, it is important to note that *the work*, that is the secret removal and then replacement of cards into the deck responsible for altering the outcome of the deal, takes place when the spectator is not looking. The four red cards are removed from the deck *before* the trick starts—at least from the point of view of the spectator and are then added to the discards well *before* the trick is performed a second time. When the heat is on, there is nothing to see. This is important.

You may recall Thomas Edison's formula for success from Chapter One, which states in essence that success comes to those who perspire. Well, removing four red cards from the deck before the audience believes the trick has started is one way to reduce perspiration. It is also a perfect metaphor for business. The Advantage

Play executive knows that the primary technique to reduce stress and strain is preparation. If you want your presentation to look magical, complete your preparations well beforehand. You can then devote all of your energy toward selling the power of *the effect*, or in the case of business, the power of *the solution*.

Now, place the deck of cards aside and turn your attention to your own business. Pick out an effect, that is a task you believe your enterprise performs satisfactorily. Apply the same analysis outlined for *Miraskill*. What does the customer, client, or colleague perceive? How does the enterprise achieve the objective? Why does it work? Finally, review the task in light of The Mechanics of Problem Solving and see if you can deliver a more efficient solution. You may be surprised at the result. Now, just think of what would happen if you applied the technique to a task that your enterprise does not perform well. Magic.

ADVANTAGE PLAY

1. The starting point for all magic is *the effect.*
2. For an *effect* to be effective, you must describe it in one simple sentence.
3. Separate *the effect*—what appears to happen— from the methodology—what really happens.
4. If you do not challenge assumptions about your strategic approach to the problem, you may work very hard and never discover the solution.
5. There are always many ways to achieve each *effect* or objective.
6. Establish a minimum quota for ideas and generate that quota by challenging all assumptions about what is or is not possible before trying to evaluate the ideas. Do not assume that a problem can be solved in the same manner as a previous problem. In an ever-changing world, every problem is unique.
7. The most valuable asset in any organization is the people who can determine the best course of action.
8. Use your inventory of experience to determine the best course of action and sell the idea.
9. To implement your solution, brief the client on the mechanics of solving the problem.
10. Failure is only a mistake if you learn nothing from it.

CHAPTER FOUR

Manufacturing Ideas

Advantages that are bound to ultimately give a percentage in favor of the professional are absolutely essential to his existence...

S. W. ERDNASE

ADVANTAGE PLAY IS ALSO ABOUT, well, advantages. In a casino environment, some blackjack players attempt to gain an advantage over the house by counting cards; that is they use a system to track the value of cards that have been played in order to provide a more accurate evaluation of the value of the cards that are still in play and the odds of receiving those cards. Others look for *tells*, the psychological or physiological signs that indicate innermost thoughts. Creative problem solvers enhance the odds for success by cultivating advantages. This chapter examines two techniques that provide the Advantage Player with an advantage.

Some may take offense with my attempt to demystify the creative process. Many argue that the source of artistic creation springs from the subconscious mind, a place that despite psychoanalysis, mere mortals can never completely comprehend. These are usually the same people who recognize only the arts as creative endeavors. I am not sure why people promulgate this idea. Perhaps they derive comfort in the notion that they will always have an excuse should they not be able to produce a timely solution. Advantage Players do not have this luxury.

The most creative person I have known personally was Stewart James, the creator of *Miraskill*. Stewart was born on May 14, 1908, in the small village of Courtright, Ontario, near what would eventually become the large petroleum-refining center of Sarnia, Ontario. The youngest child of three—and only son—of eccentric yet strict Presbyterian parents, his formative years involved great hardship but sowed the seeds for his creative output. I met Stewart late in his life, around 1980, and remained his friend until he passed away in 1996. It is in honor of our close relationship that I call him Stewart.

Stewart was the most prolific inventor of magic in the twentieth century. Where most magicians invent a handful of magic routines during the course of their lives, Stewart created over one thousand. His prodigious output has been recorded in two mammoth publications totaling over 2,700 pages. His life and work, particularly the correspondence he left behind, provide insight into not only what it means to be creative but also how one can improve proficiency at problem solving. This chapter explores two techniques he used regularly: *The Creative Infrastructure* and *Idea Kindlers*, and how they can help the Advantage Play executive manufacture creative solutions.

The Creative Infrastructure

The Creative Infrastructure is an organized repository of personal and professional resources that creates an inventory of experience from which one can generate ideas and evaluate options. It consists of at least three sub-systems: a mental and physical state that fosters creativity; a system for storing, retrieving, and sharing information; and a system that encourages mentorship. Advantage Play executives regard The Creative Infrastructure as another piece of machinery that can help an enterprise fabricate solutions. The machinery needs to be created or acquired, maintained, and managed if it is going to be an asset that generates returns. Let's examine each sub-system in more detail.

The power of positive thinking is well documented. A positive mindset or approach to creative problem solving is equally important. Stewart James had definite thoughts about the creative process—thoughts that made each search for an elusive principle, idea, or solution a rewarding experience. First, he believed that all answers or solutions pre-exist in the world. You just have to discover them.

Stewart developed this notion in 1915 or 1916, when he discovered *Boy's World*—a magazine for youth published in America and distributed through church groups across North America. This magazine published a series of magic tricks under the byline of Howard Thurston— North America's reigning Master Magician. One trick in particular—a simple rope trick entitled Knot of Enchantment—inspired Stewart to search for principles inherent in the world that if repeated would create apparently impossible results each and every time. His own discovery, *Miraskill*, is a perfect example. Despite the initial shuffling and dealing procedure, the same result occurs every time. Once Stewart realized that such principles exist like unknown stars in a galaxy waiting to be discovered, he became not just a child pretending to be on a great adventure, but a real explorer on a real adventure. Stewart adopted the mindset of an *explorer* rather than that of an *inventor.*

Second, Stewart regarded the creative process as a journey to a destination in the mind. Both the journey and the final destination were real to him even though the exercise was conducted purely in the imagination. The journey always started on an avenue of thought grounded in the real world because Stewart believed that every new or underutilized idea could be traced to a nucleus of familiar knowledge. It is the task of the creative person to explore on this journey the untapped potential or principles inherent in the knowledge. He named this place where all solutions exist *The Other Place*—a repository of principles inherent in nature that, once discovered and applied, could make any problem disappear. Advantage Play executives recognize that ideas and solutions are precious metals waiting to be discovered, staked, and mined. They pre-exist in our world. One must allocate the resources to finding them and harvesting their potential.

Third, Stewart believed that this creative journey was undertaken in *partnership* with the mind. He regarded his mind as a separate entity making the journey with him. He did this not only to track how he was thinking but also what he was thinking. As a partner in the creative process, the mind can take and make suggestions. Stewart developed this mindset to facilitate the dialogue between the conscious mind and the subconscious. The dialogue is required to create combinations or innovations that you might never conceive in consciousness.

You must talk to yourself. You cannot force ideas into the brain because forced ideas only come back as memories, not innovations.

Fourth, Stewart rejected the notion that this creative dialogue occurred at only certain periods of the day. A minister of the church, one of the few people with whom Stewart discussed his concept of creativity, used to track the times of his creative output in his diary. The minister tried to predict from that data in which periods he was more likely to generate a creative idea. People do this today. Some state that they are a "morning person" or that they "work better at night." Stewart regarded this as a negative approach to creativity. He did not want to be a passive receptacle waiting for something to drop in from mental space. He wanted to be able to manufacture the creative mindset; he wanted to tap his creativity on demand.

Fifth, Stewart knew from first-hand experience the danger associated with being an independent thinker. As a child, he was rarely allowed outside to play. In fact, because playing with other children was forbidden, he improvised. He would place a barrel of rocks on the end of a plank as his counterweight on the seesaw. Other children would laugh at him. Although the ridicule he experienced as a child, both from the other children who laughed at his antics and from his parents who seemed to do everything to make his life miserable, forced Stewart to seek refuge in his imagination, he was strong enough to contemplate, explore, and thrive in this world. Most people in business do not have his fortitude. They retreat in the face of criticism, concealing their thoughts in order to escape criticism.

Negative thinking in the business world can manifest itself in many forms. You probably have seen a colleague make a sarcastic remark toward another colleague's suggestion, perhaps even one of your own, thereby nipping all discussion and creativity in the bud. Most react by withdrawing from the discussion, if not physically then mentally. This negative mindset has an impact on every level in an organization. I have witnessed a large cultural institution crippled by its board of trustees interfering so much in the day-to-day operations that employees were afraid to submit any new suggestions to management or perform any tasks that threatened the status quo because they feared their ideas or work would be negated. The institution became impoverished instead of empowered.

Advantage Play executives understand the role and place of criticism. They recognize the danger of negative thinking and do everything within their power to convert it into something positive. Instead of eliminating criticism, they try to harness it by channeling it to its proper time and place. They understand that criticism belongs in the third stage of The Mechanics of Problem Solving. Advantage Play executives who lead or participate in meetings also recognize the importance of the free flow of ideas during the idea generation stage and counter criticism by asserting that such criticism may be valid, but not at this time. It is important to recognize where critical thinking belongs in the problem-solving process. The Mechanics of Problem Solving is a roadmap that suggests a course of action and specific techniques to determine that particular time and place.

Stewart also advocated creating a positive environment

for creative problem solving. He called this *The Inner Sanctum*. The Inner Sanctum housed two things. First, it was home to his collection of books, magazines, and correspondence with an accompanying filing system and index. Second, and equally important, it contained a host of personalities who could assist him with his endeavors. These personalities were his books, his desk, and even the washroom. Just as a person may have a special name for his or her pet, Stewart bestowed pet names on any article, place, or object he considered a favorite. His notebook, in which he compiled odd arithmetical principles, was named Matthew, although he usually just abbreviated the name to Math. His writing table was named Mark. Stewart said that regardless of the subject he was working on, he only had to pull his chair forward to know that he was getting closer to the Mark. The books in his reference library were called Luke because when he was uncertain as to whether an idea had appeared in print, he would go to Luke in his library. Stewart even added a mental twist to the washroom, which, like many of us, he called John. He described John as a terrific poker play. Whenever it was needed, he always ended up with a flush!

Office managers, designers, and ergonomically minded engineers are now reshaping the work environment to make it more conducive to manufacturing ideas. Techniques include encouraging casual attire on Fridays, constructing non-territorial workstations in open concept offices, and placing pinball machines and other amusements at strategic locations to spell the conscious mind while the unconscious mind enjoins the "ideation" process. All contribute to creating a positive environment for creative problem solving.

The second sub-system in The Creative Infrastructure is the system that allows you to store, access, and share information. As the starting point on the creative journey involves discovering as much about the problem you are working on from the past, information becomes critical. One of the reasons David Copperfield became the foremost illusionist of the twentieth century is because he has amassed a very significant collection of materials. In 1991, he paid $2,100,000 (U.S.) for the Mulholland Collection of magic books and related ephemera, outbidding the United States Library of Congress. He added to this shortly afterward by purchasing several other large collections. These collections now form David Copperfield's International Museum and Library of the Conjuring Arts—a private museum housed in his enormous warehouse in a location somewhere in Nevada.

Copperfield's acquisition of rare books, apparatus, and memorabilia assist him and his creative team in generating new material. There is no need to look at a blank page and wait for inspiration when there are thousands of volumes chock-full of ideas waiting to be adapted for a new audience and any modern medium. Advantage Play executives know that The Creative Infrastructure must act as a reservoir of information that can spark ideas.

An important aspect of The Creative Infrastructure is how you organize this information. The information available to us is expanding exponentially. A person in North America on average may read hundreds of newspapers and dozens of magazines; listen to or watch hundreds of hours of radio or television; buy numerous books and CDs; fill out thousands of notices, forms, and memos; and spend over sixty hours on the telephone in the course of a year. That is a great deal of information and doesn't include the World Wide Web. The Advantage Player must design a sub-system not only to alleviate Information Anxiety (a term coined by the futurist Richard Saul Wurman that describes the anxiety one feels at being overwhelmed by information one is unfamiliar with or only superficially aware of), but also to foster personal growth and the ability to solve problems.

Of course, it is not the quantity of information that is important as much as the manner in which you store, track, and retrieve the information. Stewart James did not have the technology to manipulate large amounts of information. He knew how to harvest the best from the information that he did possess and he designed his own filing and index system to help him record, track, and retrieve information for his personal use. He placed all his magazines in one pile as they arrived until he had a chance to read them and index items of interest. His system for tracking information was quite simple. He would take a full sheet of writing paper, fold it in four and use it as a bookmark. When he found something worth noting, he would enter the reference on the bookmark. As the bookmark was folded from a full sheet of paper, it was substantial in size and not easily misplaced. When he had a number of references and a bit of time, he would transfer his bookmark entries to a master index. The master index consisted of file cards.

Stewart said that his filing and indexing system made him approach reading with a different perspective. Each periodical offered hours of enjoyment and a possible path to that most rewarding of all thoughts—a new idea.

Further, his indexing system also helped him to determine the value of the various publications he received. Material he decided he could use in whole or in part went on file. The systematic recording had its value. By comparing the amount of material listed from all the magazines he received in a particular year, he could instantly tell which one was the most valuable. By checking the material filed from a magazine one year with the amount filed the previous year, he could judge whether or not that magazine was improving.

The practice of law is also about access to secrets. It is advanced library science. Legal secrets are buried in statutes, case law, articles, and reports. It is up to the Advantage Play lawyer to access this information and provide the client with the best possible advice. Fortunately computers have made tracking and accessing information that much easier. Whether you use a bookmark to track ideas for later data entry or build up an extensive filing cabinet or database of ideas, your time will be rewarded. Each Advantage Player must build his or her own personal Creative Infrastructure and do so one piece at a time.

One aspect of the practice of law I came to appreciate was the circulation of information. Anytime anyone in our firm came across an article that was germane to our practice, a copy of the article would be circulated through the department and all the lawyers were encouraged to note or copy it and add it to their personal Creative Infrastructures. As each member of the department contributed material over time, the firm's level of knowledge grew exponentially. It was also a wonderful way to start a conversation over lunch, in a hallway, or at a conference. The exchange of information leads to the third sub-section of The Creative Infrastructure—mentorship.

The most important component in a Creative Infrastructure is people. It is vital to form relationships with people with whom you can exchange information, learn new ideas from, and obtain comments on existing intelligence. Every sorcerer needs his apprentice and every apprentice needs his sorcerer. It is a symbiotic relationship. Unfortunately many executives still attempt to go it alone either because they believe in the notion of being self-made, or they do not know how to foster profitable relationships.

Very few successful people are really self-made. It is a self-deceptive illusion. Success comes to those who learn from others. Good role models abound. Dai Vernon, for example, was quick to attribute much of his success to his own mentors. Although he appreciated whatever advice they would bestow during these brief encounters (a little encouragement can go a long way), he was inspired more than anything by seeing their performances. On occasion he would take a formal lesson. But most of the time the exchange of information was on an ad hoc basis. Both are important. Vernon wrote:

> *For the beginner, the main psychological advantage of taking lessons is the stimulus he gets from a source he respects, until he can find the stimulus within himself. Remember, every expert once started as a student who gradually assimilated his own concepts, and tested methods and ideas of presentation, mostly learned from false starts and failure, as well as from success, until he developed his*

knowledge and ability through hard work and enthusi-
asm. The most celebrated artist and his most
inexperienced student work with exactly the same raw
materials. All that the teacher can do is give the student
these reliable tools, and he must learn how to use them.*

The distance between the student and the teacher
need not be the determinative factor. In August 1947, for
example, Stewart James received a letter from a sixteen-
year-old enthusiast located in a remote part of
Canada—Moose Jaw, Saskatchewan. The letter states in
part:

Dear Mr. James:

I know this is a very bold thing to do, but I am writing this
letter in the hope that you would like to correspond with a
boy that is absolutely crazy over magic . . . I have been
using your Miraskill and Remembering the Future since I
came across them. What puzzles me is how you come
across such unusual principles. Is it by chance or by read-
ing something that brings them to mind?

*   In closing, Mr. James, I do hope you will at least try*
corresponding with me for a while. Since I came here a
year or so ago from Galt, Ontario, I haven't come across a
single magician. And to me that is a fate worse than death.
I live, breath [sic], eat and sleep magic; when school work
and magic clash, as you might imagine, magic is always
the victor.

Hopefully yours,
Allan Slaight

---

* Vernon, Dai, "The Vernon Touch," *Genii*, Vol. 33, No. 3, November, 1968,
Los Angeles, CA, page 112.

Stewart's response, in part, was:

Dear Allan:

I am sure that we are going to be friends and my friends call me Stewart.

> *Yes, I will correspond with you if you will agree not to be annoyed if my reply is sometimes delayed. My business makes most exacting demands upon me at intervals and for many years I have corresponded regularly with several magicians. Their letters naturally have priority. Make new friends but keep the old.*

> *[On Creativity] Maybe the first hundred times you don't succeed. This is important. Retain your notes. Don't throw them away. This is the mistake so many make. Look them over from time to time. You never forget, you only fail to remember and so, quite unknown to you, your sub-conscious has remained working. Sleep is the royal road to the sub-conscious so read your notes before you go to sleep.*

> *Remind me when you write again if you want me to describe step by step how I worked out some tricks.*

Good Hunting!

Stewart James

Despite the difference in age and geographic location, this initial exchange ignited a personal relationship that would last for almost fifty years. Allan Slaight would grow from being a sixteen-year-old child obsessed with magic to a Canadian media mogul, the international authority on Stewart James, and an accomplished performer of magic. Stewart taught, challenged, and cajoled Allan Slaight. Allan persuaded Stewart to explain his magic and articulate his theories. Both profited enormously from the relationship—and the distinctive advantages of Advantage Play.

Sometimes someone must *broker* the Sorcerer and Apprentice relationship. I will always be indebted to P. Howard Lyons, a brilliant magic thinker, jazz expert, publisher of science fiction fanzines, and well-respected accountant, for brokering my relationship with my main magical mentor, Ross Bertram. For many years Howard organized a four-day conference for magicians at a beautiful resort in Niagara-On-The-Lake, Ontario. Admission was by invitation only and invitations were restricted to thirty inventive performers. The conference program consisted of three gourmet meals a day, an open bar, and few scheduled events. Delegates wandered from the restaurant to the bar exchanging tricks, anecdotes, and information with other like-minded individuals. I was invited to attend when I was quite young, not because I was a particularly inventive performer, but because Howard believed that it was important to broker knowledge. Each attendee had a roommate. Mine was Ross Bertram, who was one of the great and most reclusive sleight-of-hand artists of the twentieth century. Ross and I hit it off, and shortly after the conference finished, I started the weekly visits to his home that altered the course of my life.

Zen philosophy states that the master will appear when the student is ready. How then does the master know when the student is ready? The master knows the student is ready by the questions the student asks. Asking the right questions is critical. The nature of the question reveals the level of understanding the student has attained on the subject matter and the guidance the student requires to progress. If the student shows familiarity with the work, he or she deserves a more measured and helpful response. The student who identifies the issues deserves appropriate guidance. True masters respond because they remember the time when they themselves received such guidance.

The Sorcerer and Apprentice relationship is a two way street. For even though the student may feel indebted to the master for imparting wisdom, the master also benefits from the relationship. The master will develop new insight into *the work* because he or she will be forced to articulate the same concept several different ways until it is thoroughly understood by the student. By continually translating the thought until it registers, the master achieves a greater understanding of the craft.

Most progressive corporate organizations now promote mentor-protégé relationships. Law firms partner senior practitioners with juniors. Many companies partner women who have achieved success with younger women who may fear it is impossible to break through "the glass ceiling." The relationships need not be formal. If on a unique transaction, it is easy to invite a junior to participate to show them what makes the transaction unique, challenging, and exciting.

Just as it is incumbent on the mentor to look for the protégé, it is up to the protégé to seek the mentor. He or she must excel at assigned work and seek out those challenges that require greater expertise without being obtrusive. The protégé must expect to pay the price of added effort. The price is usually undertaking additional work without economic compensation. The reward is the exposure to more sophisticated work and technique and a valuable contact becoming part of the protégé's Creative Infrastructure.

One can create a temporary mentor-protégé relationship in a controlled setting in order to profit from the dynamic. For example, one of my clients was a major toy distributor who had to introduce a new product line to the sales force each season. To do so, they would assemble the sales force from across the country and, like most companies, throw them into a conference setting and let them look at the sixty-plus new products that they had to sell in their respective territories. I suggested a different approach.

I divided the sales staff into smaller units. Each unit consisted of six to eight representatives, composed of junior and senior staff culled from different areas of the country and market demographics. Each group was given six products in the new line. Each unit was required to generate sales ideas, approaches, or markets for each product and table their suggestions in a memorandum. A spokesperson in each group was required to stand, introduce a product and offer one suggestion that could help move the product. Not only did the entire sales force develop a personal awareness of the new product line in an extremely short period of time, the memoranda were collated and redistributed so that each individual could profit from the collective experience of the group. The memoranda gave them leverage. Archimedes, the purported inventor of the lever, when questioned about the power of his invention said, "Give me a place to stand and I will move the earth." Leverage is such a powerful concept that if one could figure out where to stand and had a plank long enough positioned over an appropriate fulcrum, one could indeed move the earth. A Creative Infrastructure is the lever that properly managed allows the Advantage Player to do the same.

Idea Kindlers

To generate a sufficient quantity of ideas during the second stage of The Mechanics of Problem Solving, the Advantage Play executive must challenge all assumptions. This can be difficult because of our habitual reliance on logical reasoning. Stewart James developed a variety of techniques at an early age to help him challenge assumptions and develop insight into difficult problems. He called these techniques *Idea Kindlers*. Idea Kindlers not only assisted Stewart in solving problems but also provided him with a key to unlocking the subconscious.

In order to generate ideas, it is helpful to visualize, like Stewart, the process of generating ideas as a journey. Like a tourist who leaves a point of departure on a journey toward a final destination—a creative solution—the Advantage Play executive must not be afraid to explore the side streets. Every new idea encountered on these side streets increases the horizon of the mind and its capacity to explore new ideas.

The starting point for the journey is the *Point of Departure*. Many executives fail to consider the Point of Departure, preferring instead to set off toward the solution as quickly as possible. They assume they are familiar with the place they are leaving. Stewart rarely made this assumption. For him, the Point of Departure was an integral part of the journey. It could reveal much about the final destination and the path to it. As every avenue of thought is based on a nucleus of familiar knowledge, the Advantage Play executive explores the untapped potential and principles inherent in this knowledge and learns everything about the place he or she is leaving before embarking on the journey.

Most executives, for example, would not alter the physical plant of an operation without noting when it was established, examining its current condition, and developing a floor plan of the plant. It's like checking the foundation of a house and correcting or replacing any deficiencies before adding an extension. The Advantage Play executive takes the same approach to generating ideas by making the effort to know the past, the present, and the future of the idea he or she wishes to discover.

The *Trinity* is an important concept in all of Stewart's creative endeavors. By viewing each problem in terms of a triangle instead of a straight line, Stewart forced his mind off the linear page. Ideas could be ignited by the sparks that generated from either of the other two points of the triangle. Stewart maintained that one must always be prepared to approach a problem from any angle—a "TRY-angle."

A good place to start an exploration for ideas is the past, and Stewart always looked back before trying to move forward. He said, "If you stand at a hurdle you may not be able to jump over it. Go back a way, run, and you will probably make it. It is sometimes easier to advance by going back. By researching and exploring the less-frequented paths, the odds are much higher that hidden treasures will be found." From research comes knowledge and from knowledge comes invention. Advantage Play executives seek truth through science.

To analyze the past, it helps to put pen to paper. Create a flow chart or what Stewart would describe as *The Family Tree*. Stewart started using this particular technique from 1921 onward more than any other to organize information. In essence, he mapped out branches of thought like the trunk and branches of a tree on the basis that one idea or development led to another. Obviously, it is possible to extend the branches to infinity, but knowing more and more about less and less would not be of great utility. Draw on your Creative Infrastructure to provide content and then prune the tree to give it shape. The purpose is to capture and trace the development of problems and ideas.

Once you understand the nature and history of the problem you are trying to solve, it is time to use Idea Kindlers to help you challenge the assumptions your logical reasoning skills have made about solving the problem. Over the course of his lifetime, Stewart developed twenty-one different idea generation techniques, each of which bore a colorful name: *Strange Partners and Unrecorded Deeds, Too Many Cooks and Saving The Broth*, and *Bouncing Thoughts off a Turning Glass*. Stewart wrote the name of each one of twenty-one thought-starters on a file card. The cards were not placed in any particular order because they had no lasting relationship to one another. He would shuffle the cards, turn one face up, and then try to apply the approach suggested on that card to the problem at hand. If unsuccessful, he would reshuffle the cards and turn up a different card to see what that particular technique could motivate. It was an arbitrary, mechanical approach to kick-starting creative solutions.

We will examine now four of these Idea Kindlers—*Grafter and the Tree of Knowledge, Twelve Keys To All From The Pyramids, The Vision of Ezekiel,* and *Three Companions Who Never Were*—in detail to give you a sense of the technique and their potential application for the Advantage Play executive.

GRAFTER AND THE TREE OF KNOWLEDGE

Grafter and the Tree of Knowledge is the first cousin of The Family Tree. Stewart James developed numerous Family Trees for creative journeys he took throughout his lifetime. Collectively these trees stood in what he called an orchard in the land of *The Waiting Place For Unborn Thoughts*. The concept of Grafter And The Tree Of Knowledge is quite simple. When there was no suitable branch on The Family Tree that could kindle an idea, Stewart would examine his orchard, select an appropriate branch from another tree and graft it on to another. He would look for what developed.

This technique can easily be applied in the business environment. First, develop a series of flowcharts for various operations. This need not be done in one sitting. They could be created over time and stored in the physical equivalent of Stewart's The Waiting Place For Unborn Thoughts. To generate ideas, remove one set of branches from one flowchart and paste it onto another. Do not dismiss it because it does not immediately bear fruit, so to speak. Mull it over and see what associations develop—associations that lead to new ideas. Remember the concept of play in Advantage Play. The goal in the idea generation phase of The Mechanics of Problem Solving is to challenge assumptions and explore the possibilities. Suspend judgment until stage three of the process. If nothing materializes, try the next technique.

TWELVE KEYS TO ALL FROM THE PYRAMIDS

This Idea Kindler was inspired by a marking said to be in one of the pyramids that suggested that it takes twelve men to make one perfect man. Stewart made a list of twelve people including himself and then viewed the problem as it might be worked out by each person in turn. Stewart kept a biographical dictionary close at hand to help him nominate others for this task. He would flip through the pages and decide to invite one of the entries to join his working group. He tried to insure that each of the eleven—he was the twelfth—had a different occupation or skill from the others. Stewart maintained that the breakthrough came when you decided not to limit yourself to one field but to use the broad canvas of all worlds.

This Idea Kindler is of great assistance for Advantage Play executives. You already may have applied this technique unconsciously in your own work. Many executives, for example, use their imagination to visualize how a colleague or friend they admire will react to a piece of work. The aim is always to profit from the advice—real or imaginary. James just expanded the circle. He sought the advice of a *Virtual Board of Directors* rather than one trusted friend. I find this technique particularly useful. My board is composed of people with great powers of persuasion, superb technical understanding of minutiae, and the ability to express complex thoughts with great clarity. I consult with them in my imagination and try to profit from their experience. It's like having a board of directors available to you 24/7 without incurring the cost of the meetings or the directors' fees. If this technique fails to generate ideas, try the next one.

THE VISION OF EZEKIEL

Stewart developed this, his most abstract and sophisticated idea generation technique, after reading a passage in the Bible (Ezekiel 1:16). He imagined three wheels—each with seven spokes—floating in the air in front of him. The wheels—he called them *Ezekiel Wheels*—spun back and forth. Each wheel represented a category of a Trinity and was assigned the name based on information from his Creative Infrastructure or Family Tree. Each spoke in each wheel would be labeled accordingly, usually with a Point of Departure related to the category the wheel represented in the Trinity. Again, Stewart would use The Family Tree to help locate names for the spokes. As the wheels were projected outward, he could turn the wheels back and forth with his mind like a master safecracker turning the tumblers in an old fashioned safe. When the rims met, there would be a "click"—a collision of ideas. This co-incidence more often than not would create the necessary spark or insight worth further exploration. Although he could control the movement of the wheels with his mind,

Stewart usually recorded the names of the wheels and the spokes on paper in the form of three disks, which he would lay flat on the table before him.

Occasionally, he would use twenty-one cards instead of disks with spokes. He wrote the names of six objects—one object to a card, on six of the cards. On another six cards he wrote the names of six effects or objectives, again one to a card. The next six cards bore the names of six methods—one to a card. The three remaining cards were left blank. He then placed a single dot on the back of each *object* card, two dots on the back of each *effect* card and three dots on the back of each *method* card. One, two and three dots were placed on the backs of the three blank cards respectively.

Stewart would then gather the cards, shuffle them, and deal them face down in three piles, placing all the single-dotted cards in the first pile, all double-dotted cards in the second pile and all triple-dotted cards in the third pile. He would then turn the top card of each pile face up to reveal the name of an *object*, *effect*, and *method*. He considered this his starting point for the problem at hand. He would discard these three cards if the combination did not suggest an avenue for exploration and then turn up the next three top cards, repeating this process until he was able to produce a combination that had potential.

Occasionally Stewart would then extend The Vision of Ezekiel by adding aspects from Twelve Keys to All from the Pyramids. He prepared seven more cards, each bearing the name of a famous person or occupation other than magician. After turning the three cards representing the wheels face up, he would turn over a card from this last group and imagine how the person or occupation could influence his thinking.

This technique is particularly useful in Advantage Play to explore the untapped potential in an existing product or service relationship, or to forge a new liaison that may be mutually profitable.

When Stewart was young, he would send away for the catalogues of magical wares distributed by a magic shop, page after page of which described the most fantastic miracles for sale. Stewart would use the catalogue descriptions as a Point of Departure for his imagination to create his own way of achieving each *effect*. Other times, wanting to outwit his father who, afraid that his son would be able to do something that he himself could not explain would open all the magic tricks Stewart was able to purchase in order to learn the secret to the effect prior to passing them on to Stewart, Stewart would develop new magical effects for existing apparatus.

So, how does this apply to Manufacturing Ideas and Advantage Play? Take, for example, seven products or services that you offer your customers or clients. Write the name of each one on a card. Take another seven cards and write the names of seven different modes of distribution. Now, write the seven different questions suggested by the mnemonic S.C.A.M.P.E.R. Substitute. Combine. Adapt. Modify. Put to Other Uses. Eliminate. Reverse or Rearrange. You have created a deck of twenty-one cards that can be marked, shuffled, and dealt as Stewart did with his cards. Turn over the top card of each pile and see if the combination sparks an idea. You can add a fourth pile of seven cards bearing the names of the people on your Virtual Board of Directors to see what they can add to the exercise.

The method and utility of this technique may be difficult to visualize initially. It does require one to suspend logical reasoning and visualize abstract, non-linear ideas and images. It requires practice. Stewart became so good at it that eventually he was able to conduct the entire exploration without pen and paper. He conducted the entire procedure and tracked the results purely in his mind, afraid that if he always put his thoughts down on paper, over time he might need paper and pencil to think.

For most of us, however, creating cue cards, flow-charts, family trees, or mapping the procedure out on paper is a good idea. Stewart suggested it was like a child who uses training wheels while learning to ride a bicycle. The training wheels are a stopgap measure until the child develops a sense of balance and performs that activity without conscious effort. Undoubtedly it is helpful to commit ideas to paper, particularly if you are going to share your ideas with others.

We will conclude our exploration of Stewart's Idea Kindlers by examining his most personal and productive approach to idea generation. Extremely simple in concept and execution, it is one of the most effective ways to tap the subconscious.

THREE COMPANIONS WHO NEVER WERE

Stewart's most prolific technique—and the one he was most reluctant to discuss—bore several names including *Three Companions Who Never Were*, *At The Talking Table* and *The Deepsters*. The technique, like the names, evolved over time. It started when Stewart conjured up an imaginary playmate as a young boy—a feat not uncommon for one of tender years. This imaginary person—named Originally but shortened later to Rigonally—became his best friend and companion. Many years passed with only Rigonally visiting him. The two others—Khardova and Faxton—joined them later and together, Stewart and his Three Companions Who Never Were explored *The Other Side*.

Stewart would initiate each session by sitting around a square of some description—a simple table or even a handkerchief would do—and the three others would join him. This square became The Talking Table. The four of them always sat in the same position with Rigonally directly across from Stewart, Khardova on his left, and Faxton on his right. When they would meet, Stewart would remain silent. He had to be prepared, though, because sometimes ideas came so quickly that he had to chalk them right on the tabletop. He knew that their suggestions would never be repeated and that if he did not get them down the first time it would be a long and painful process to reconstruct the details. Sometimes the Companions could be quite uncommunicative, sitting as a group around the table with long periods of time passing without a response. Like Twelve

Keys To All From The Pyramids, each of Three Companions Who Never Were had their own special skill. Khardova provided expertise with cards, Rigonally supplied the imagination, and Faxton was responsible for various facts. Unlike Twelve Keys, Stewart had little control over the direction or nature of the problems they would discuss. The only thing he could do was to terminate the meeting.

At this point you might be asking, how does Stewart's relationship with The Deepsters help the Advantage Player. Dr. Edward de Bono (who coined the term *lateral thinking*) proposed in one of his most innovative texts, *Six Thinking Hats*, a technique that can enhance productivity by imagining the donning and doffing of a half-dozen colored hats. In a group-think session, when you put on your green hat, you assume the mindset of being creative and fertile; when you put on your blue hat, you are cool and dispassionate; and so on—red (emotional), white (neutral), black (negative), yellow (positive). If you sit in a particular chair and don a particular hat, you accept the role of a particular kind of thinking.

This was certainly true for Stewart. Three Companions Who Never Were represented, however, more than just a wardrobe. They were friends, friends whose relationship evolved over time as their expertise grew, and friends who found strength in the depth of the relationship. It became very personal and it is this personal nature that made it a much more effective technique than colored hats. Stewart's most successful Idea Kindlers were based on the personal relationships he created with imaginary people rather than inanimate or arbitrary exercises devoid of personality.

P. Howard Lyons, who along with Allan Slaight was a pivotal liaison between Stewart, his imagination, and a wider public, believed that James used this technique to freely enter and exit his own subconscious. Stewart was much more modest. He believed that he somehow had happened on a system that worked for him as a stimulus to creativity, one that he was lucky enough to use for many years with great success. Whatever the truth may be, it worked.

Once again, it is important to place these Idea Kindlers into perspective. They are designed for a specific purpose, to assist the Advantage Play executive in challenging assumptions and discovering new insight into problems, insight that can spark potential solutions. Stewart wrote,

> I would use ANY 'gimmick'—no matter how fantastic—as long as it engenders a sensation of a partnership with the source of all knowledge. It becomes more than seeking the solution to a problem. It is the ecstatic feeling of being granted the privilege of a distant view of a perfect world where only absolutes exist...that is so magnetic in its attraction that one only dare look at it from afar or one would lose the ability of desire to retreat to our drab and, in comparison, infinitesimal outland.

All of these Idea Kindlers have historical precedents. Unbeknownst to Stewart, the thirteenth-century Spanish theologian and visionary Ramon Lull developed early logic machines that were also based on the power of the wheel, and the ancient Greeks believed that each man had his *idios daemon*, a personal spirit that could be cultivated and developed. Ever an Advantage Player, Stewart James had three. Most books on creativity now offer dozens of techniques to generate ideas. They are an accepted part of the exercise. Several titles have been listed in an appendix of this book should you wish to explore these techniques in more detail. As S. W. Erdnase wrote, "The student will need no further incentive the moment the least progress is made."

Let us conclude this discussion of Manufacturing Ideas with an observation. James was well aware that this technique bordered on madness. It was many years before Stewart disclosed the existence of his imaginary friends. Not only did he fear public ridicule but he also thought that he might lose contact with them if they were ever the subject of a published article. Further, he secretly feared that if he did disclose how he could visit The Other Place, others too would be able to find their way and he would no longer be there alone—the only person able to mine the precious principles he had discovered.

Stewart also was acutely aware that if he spent too much time in this land, he risked never finding his way back. He would often ask, "What limits the imagination?" One can project the mind only so far, and then one must use individual judgment as to when to turn back. And yet, he knew one must also be able to return to that land of imagination before being away too long, otherwise you may not be able to find your way back there either. How then does one achieve the balance? Stewart thought that the perfect being for exploring the creative was a cross between a grasshopper and a homing pigeon. He christened it a *homing hopper*. The homing hopper would permit a train of thought to dart about with the freedom of a grasshopper but with the knowledge that it will always be able return to the Point of Departure with the instinct of a homing pigeon. It is an issue for the Advantage Play executive who must encourage creativity. The trips to the subconscious must be managed like any other activity. Much will depend on the management style of the individual players within the corporate culture and the enterprise itself.

A D V A N T A G E   P L A Y

1. Creative problem solvers enhance the odds for success by cultivating advantages.
2. A Creative Infrastructure is a system of storing, retrieving, and sharing information in an environment that fosters creativity in individuals and mentors it in others.
3. Advantage Play executives build The Creative Infrastructure one element at a time. They share information so that the base level of knowledge grows exponentially.
4. It is not the quantity of information but the use you make of it that is important.
5. Very few successful people are self-made. It is an illusion. Success comes to those who learn from others. It is a symbiotic relationship.
6. The creative process is a journey to a destination undertaken in partnership with the mind. It is the role of the Advantage Player to explore on this journey the untapped potential inherent in a nucleus of familiar knowledge.
7. You cannot undertake this journey of Manufacturing Ideas unless you understand the place from where you will depart. Building on the foundation of others saves time and experimentation.
8. Do not be a passive receptacle waiting for something to drop in from mental space. Use *Idea Kindlers* to lead your mind to new stations of enlightenment.

9. Creative people need to visit the source of their creativity as frequently as possible, lest they lose touch with their muse. They must not linger in this land unnecessarily, lest they lose their way back home.

CHAPTER FIVE

The Multiple Option Universe

*This knowledge, or thorough comprehension
of the possibilities of professional card playing, can be imparted only by practical
illustration of the processes employed, and
the reader desiring a complete understanding should take the deck in hand and work
out for himself the action as it is described.*

S. W. ERDNASE

T HE PREVIOUS CHAPTER EXAMINED two devices that
provide The Advantage Play executive with a
creative edge: The Creative Infrastructure and Idea
Kindlers. This chapter examines a third device—*The
Multiple Option Universe*—that provides the Advantage
Play executive with yet another advantage. Stated simply, The Multiple Option Universe is an inventory of
solutions developed during the second stage of The
Mechanics of Problem Solving, each of which will
achieve the same effect—the solution to the problem.

There are several reasons to cultivate multiple
options. First, by developing and perfecting a variety of
methods, the Advantage Play executive can select the
best method to achieve the objective based on the conditions faced when it comes time to implement the
solution. This ability to adapt instantly to adverse market

conditions provides the Advantage Play executive with a distinct advantage over the competition. Second, multiple options make it easier to achieve repeat success—something that is becoming harder to do in this ever-changing world. Third, multiple options make it difficult for the competition to duplicate your success because the tricks of your trade are proprietary, your own.

When Dai Vernon first appeared on the New York magic scene in 1915, he quickly became renowned for fooling the very best by repeating the same effect over and over. Vernon paid little regard to the cardinal rule of magic that states the magician should never repeat the same trick twice. Conventional wisdom states that the audience has a better chance of figuring out how the trick is accomplished if the performer repeats it a second time. Audiences know what to look for and what to expect. This is why Harry Houdini was supposedly able to figure out the modus operandi behind any trick if he had the chance to see the trick performed three times. Vernon challenged this rule. For Vernon, the rule became "never perform the same trick twice for the same audience by the same method." By distinguishing *the effect* from *the method* and by never being satisfied with just one solution, Vernon was able to discover multiple ways of achieving the same objective. Magicians had an extremely difficult time reconstructing Vernon's technique because he varied it frequently without altering the effect. The variation in handling always threw the cognoscenti off the scent. As you will soon learn, it is possible to perform an *effect* without knowing which method you will use to achieve your objective until you are partway through the presentation. Three things are required to harness the power of multiple options in business.

First, you have to generate multiple options during the second stage of The Mechanics of Problem Solving in order to have something to work with later. We now know that multiple options exist for every problem. The solutions are limited only by the imagination. Most people, however, are satisfied if they just generate one solution. Many executives stop seeking solutions once the first one springs to mind. It is a mistake to rush to market in the name of expediency. Expediency is not the same as efficiency.

Second, you must develop a thorough understanding of the various options. This takes time, energy, and other resources. You cannot afford to learn the nuances of the work during the implementation stage. You must explore all aspects of the best alternate solutions prior to implementation. Dai Vernon's magic, for example, appeared effortless because he worked out the details—all the details—prior to performing *the effect*. He was then able to perform the effect with the confidence and with the grace that became known as *The Vernon Touch*.

Third, you must be patient and listen to the market to harness the true potential of the various options. Do not rush the performance. Even in the implementation stage, resist the temptation to conclude *the effect* with the first option that springs to mind. Always canvas other options before concluding the effect, as it is often the second or third option that produces the real commercial triumph. Again, patience is required, particularly when under pressure. This was the point that scored with the Toronto Raptors of the National Basketball Association when I addressed the team at their private dinner prior to the start of the 2000–2001 basketball season. I performed some magic and then spoke to the players about the concept of Advantage Play.

Professional basketball is all about Advantage Play. There are always many ways to achieve the objective: winning! A simple game plan is the cumulative effect of hundreds of apparently inconsequential details. Each player has many options. They must be patient enough under pressure to select the best option rather than the first one that presents itself on the court. You can only do this if you are confident and in control. Confidence comes from preparation, perspiration, and practice. Control comes from watching and listening to the action as it unfolds and altering the performance accordingly.

The easiest way to demonstrate the power of The Multiple Option Universe is to provide a business case study of it in performance. I will describe the presentation and then explain the technique behind *The Tossed Out Deck*, a pseudo-psychic *effect*. The explanation also provides us with the opportunity to review the main tenets of Advantage Play. Although *the effect* can be described in simple terms (the performer reads the minds of five people in the audience), I will storyboard *the effect* from the audience's point of view before explaining *how* and *why* it works.

THE TOSSED OUT DECK

"You have probably heard the expression, 'You must have read my mind!' While many people scoff at the suggestion that it is humanly possible

*for one person to know the exact thoughts of
another, others say that the mind is the last frontier—an untapped universe where anything is
possible if it is unfettered—that is to say, allowed
to act naturally or instinctively. Let me demonstrate."* The performer displays a deck of cards.

*"First, we need a common language. In order
to be transferred from one mind to the other, each
thought must be unequivocal. A deck of cards is
really a self-contained language. If someone told
you that he was thinking of the five of clubs, you
would know exactly what he meant. With fifty-two
cards available, there is enough selection to provide variety for purposes of our demonstration.*

*"To prevent any manipulation of the cards, I
will wrap the deck with an elastic band and toss
the deck into the audience. Whoever receives the
deck, open it up and look at a card. You could, of
course, just look at the card on the bottom of the
deck—in this case the ace of spades—but it would
be kind of obvious. You are free, however, to do as
you wish. As soon as you have looked at a card,
toss the deck back to me so that I can toss it to others in the audience. Here we go."* The deck is
tossed back and forth between the performer and
five different participants, each of whom notes a
particular card in the deck. The deck is tossed
back to the performer.

*"I must now separate those of you who are
thinking of a card from those of you who are not.
If you are thinking of a card, please stand in front
of your chair. If you are not thinking of a card,*

please remain seated. It is important that those who have looked at a card remain standing because in a few moments I will ask you to concentrate on the name of your card and send me your thoughts. It is much easier to receive your thoughts if they are traveling above the heads of your peers.

"Now, please concentrate on the name of your card. Say it over and over in your mind as if it was your own personal mantra. Good! I'm getting very distinct images. I'm getting the eight of hearts, the king of clubs, the three of diamonds, the ten of spades and . . . the two . . . the two of . . . HEARTS. If I named the card you were thinking of, please sit down." The five participants return to their seats. *"Thank you very much."*

This routine was created originally by a psychic entertainer named David Hoy and was first published in 1963 in a small manuscript, *The Bold and Subtle Miracles of Dr. Faust.* The principle of deception that David Hoy employed, however, goes much further back in time. This trick is a classic example of simplicity masking a sophisticated solution. Although it may appear to be simple conceptually, there are many details that must be attended to or the illusion will fail. Now we will examine why the trick works and what it illustrates about Advantage Play. This will be followed by the analysis of how *the effect* can be enhanced by The Multiple Option Universe.

I can read the minds of five members of the audience because I *force* each participant to think of the same card—or in this case—cards. This is the same principle that was used in *Sleep on It*—the first trick explained in this book. I can force the cards because the deck I use for this demonstration just consists, in essence, of five cards—the eight of hearts, the king of clubs, the three of diamonds, the ten of spades and the two of hearts. The five force cards are repeated ten times in rotation to create what is called a *cyclical stack*. I said "in essence" because I place a different card, the ace of spades, on the bottom of the deck to mask the bottom card of the cyclical stack.

Once I establish the premise of reading minds, I remove the stacked deck from my pocket. I can spread the cards from hand to hand with the faces of the cards towards the audience without fear of an audience member noticing the fact that the bank of five cards is repeated throughout the deck. I do this casually. I close the deck, remove an elastic band from my pocket and wrap it around the deck. **(Photograph 5)** The motivation for the elastic is to band the deck together so that it may be tossed into the audience without fear of the cards separating and cascading to the floor. Most audience members are relieved that the deck is

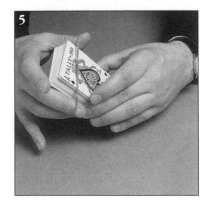

wrapped with the elastic because they assume that the elastic prohibits me from manipulating the cards with sleight of hand. In reality, the elastic is placed around the pack to prohibit the participants from examining the cards. Without the elastic, each spectator would probably spread the cards between their hands and exclaim, "Hey, they are all the same!"

Once the deck has been secured, I explain to the audience what each participant must do. I demonstrate the procedure with the deck in hand. Each spectator is requested to open the deck at one end and look at a card. **(Photograph 6)** He or she is then to toss the deck back to me. I mention that each spectator could, of course, just look at the bottom card, the ace of spades, but caution it would be quite obvi-

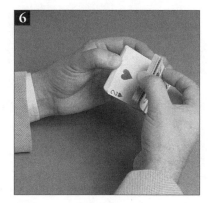

ous. This is a psychological gambit to steer each participant away from thinking of the ace of spades. Drawing attention to its position discounts the value of the card because each participant realizes that I already know the identity and location of that card. With the audience briefed, I toss the deck to the first participant and instruct him or her with words and gestures to peek at a card. The spectator will follow my lead.

I then motion for the deck to be returned to me. I do this for two reasons. First, even though the deck will be passed to others, I want to choose whom those others will be. Second, by soliciting the participation of someone close to me, I am in a better position to control the pace or timing of the selection process. I do not want the participants to spend an inordinate amount of time handling the deck. Even though the participant is free to look at any card, I retain control over the procedure. The average person will assume the deck is an ordinary one consisting of fifty-two different cards. Each participant who opens the pack to look at a card will only see, however, one of five cards. Once five people in different parts of the audience have each looked at a card, I place the deck away in my pocket and ask the participants to stand.

From the audience's point of view, the trick is just beginning. The audience assumes that the demonstration of mindreading commences as soon as I ask each participant to stand in front of his or her chair. From my point of view, however, the trick is virtually over. I must listen to the audience and deliver the best presentation available to me in the most effective manner.

The participants are asked to concentrate on the chosen cards. In reality, I know that each participant can only be thinking of one of five cards, that is one of the five cards represented in the cyclical bank of cards. With dramatic flair, I name the five cards—the eight of hearts, the king of clubs, the three of diamonds, the ten of spades and the two of hearts—and instruct the participants to sit down if I named their selection. *Five people sit down.* The audience assumes that there is a one-to-one correlation between the names of the cards and the spectators who sit down. I step forward and accept the applause.

You can see that by asking each participant to stand in front of his or her chair before rattling off the names of the five variables in the deck and then asking them to sit down if I correctly identified the cards that they were thinking of, I can create the impression—*the effect*—that I have read the minds of each individual participant. Remember that I only ask the participants to sit down after I have run through all of the variables. As each person returns to his or her seat, each participant and the audience as a whole assume that each participant thought of a different card and that I was able to divine the identity of each particular card. Nothing could be further from the truth.

People remember *The Tossed Out Deck* because *the effect* is direct and easy to describe: the performer reads the minds of members of the audience. The audience assumes that everything is above board, so to speak, because I use what appears to be an ordinary deck of cards. The deck is secured by an elastic band to prevent manipulation, and each participant gets to make his or her selection with the deck in his or her own hands. Finally, the audience's acute logical reasoning skills create the magic. The audience assumes that the five cards that I mention belong to five different people.

The power for *the effect* can be strengthened considerably if I explore other options. Let's assume that instead of naming five playing cards and expecting five people to sit down, I name only four of the five cards—the eight of hearts, the king of clubs, the three of diamonds and... the ten of spades—and instruct the participants to sit down if I named their selection. This simple change in procedure creates five multiple options.

OPTION ONE— FIVE PEOPLE SIT DOWN

Even though I named only four of the five variables, five people may still sit down. The audience never notices the fact I only mentioned the names of *four* cards. Again, the audience will assume a one-to-one correlation between the cards that were named and the thoughts of the participants. When this occurs, I step forward and accept the applause.

OPTION TWO— FOUR PEOPLE SIT DOWN

This is my favorite option. As I have named four of the five cards and four people have returned to their seats, the odds are in my favor that the remaining participant is thinking of the two of hearts as it is the only card in the deck that I have not named. I can divine the thought-of card with confidence. I instruct the participant to think of the color of his or her card. *Red!* The participant nods affirmatively. I ask them to think of the suit. *Hearts!* You can feel the dramatic tension building. Finally, I ask the participant to think of the value of the card. *A two*, I exclaim. *The two of hearts.* The participant sits down and I accept the thunderous applause.

OPTION THREE— THREE PEOPLE SIT DOWN

This option is perhaps even more effective than Option Two. As two people remaining standing, they probably are thinking of the same card—the two of hearts. I will use this knowledge to create a dramatic ending. I point to one of them and ask that person to think of the color of this mental selection. *It's a red card, correct?* I turn quickly to the other participant as if I just received her thoughts. *Yours is a red card as well—it's a heart!* I turn back to the other participant and exclaim, *Yours is also a heart!* I ask each participant to think of the value of his or her selection. Pretending to realize that both participants are thinking of the same card, I ask whether or not they know each other. Laughter. I inform the audience that the two remaining participants are both thinking of the same card. *The two of hearts!* The participants return to their seats and the audience bursts into applause.

OPTION FOUR—
TWO PEOPLE SIT DOWN

Although this may appear a less favorable scenario because I name four cards and only two people return to their seats, it can be concluded in a quick and impressive manner. After appearing somewhat puzzled with the initial response, I ask the three remaining participants to focus again on the identity of his or her selection. Feigning relief, I blurt out the identities of the three selections, *The queen of diamonds, the seven of spades and the two of hearts.* In other words, I name three cards, two of which were never in the pack, and save the one card all three people have in mind, the two of hearts, for the end. Three people sit down. The audience makes a one-to-one correlation between the three cards that I name and the three participants who sit down. The audience bursts into spontaneous applause.

OPTION FIVE—
FOUR PEOPLE SIT DOWN

At first instance, this option proceeds like Option Two. Four people sit down, one person remains standing. The difference is, however, that when I state confidently that the final participant is thinking of the two of hearts, the person does not return to his or her seat. If this scenario occurs, one of three things may have happened. First, the participant may have forgotten the identity of the initial selection. Second, the participant has decided to lie about the identity of the chosen card. Third, he or she may have chosen the ace of spades despite my initial psychological gambit. Experience has taught me, however, that it is most likely the first scenario rather than the latter. In any event, I must conclude the piece in an effective manner. I cannot simply state, for example, that the participant is a liar, remove the cyclical stack from my pocket and show the audience that the person had to be thinking of the two of hearts because it was the only unnamed card in the deck. It is not a good idea to call someone a liar even though there is strong evidence in your favor.

In this instance I remove a regular deck of cards from my other pocket and, acting somewhat surprised, ask the spectator what card he had in mind. As soon as the person names the card, let's assume the seven of diamonds, I scan the faces of the cards and state that it was impossible for the participant to select the seven of diamonds because the seven of diamonds was not even in the deck! I approach another person, reach into that person's coat pocket and remove the seven of diamonds. Thunderous applause.

By removing the regular deck of cards from my pocket, leaving the ace of spades behind, I can quickly notice the location of the participant's card in the regular deck, secretly remove it from the deck and load it into another person's jacket.

There are dozens of technical means to accomplish this task. However, if the person states that he was thinking of the ace of spades, despite my psychological gambit, I will ask the person to shuffle the regular deck. This, of course, means nothing because the ace of spades rests in my jacket pocket. I take the deck back from the person and place it into my pocket, but on a different axis than the ace. It is a simple matter for me to then reach into my pocket and conclude *the effect* by removing the ace of spades. I must confess, however, that I have never had to perform this variation. Nobody has ever thought of the ace of spades.

Even though the methodology may vary from scenario to scenario, the basic *effect* remains the same. I read the minds of members of the audience. The *effect* is effective, however, only because I took the time to learn and perfect the various options in The Multiple Option Universe prior to implementing them. Only by exploring all options that are available to achieve each objective during the idea generation stage can an Advantage Play executive truly adapt to adverse conditions. There is no time to go back to the drawing board and develop another solution. The transition from one option to another must be secret, and silent and as effortless as breathing. The audience is waiting.

A D V A N T A G E P L A Y

1. The Multiple Option Universe provides the Advantage Play executive with another advantage.
2. The Multiple Option Universe is an inventory of solutions developed during the second stage of The Mechanics of Problem Solving.
3. In an ever-changing world, you must be able to achieve the same result with a variety of methods.
4. Resist the temptation to perform the first solution that springs to mind.
5. You must explore all aspects of the best alternate solutions prior to implementation.
6. To harness the true potential of various options, you must be patient and listen to the market. You must be confident and in control.
7. Confidence comes from preparation and practice. Control comes from listening to the action as it unfolds and altering the performance accordingly.

Technology,
Innovation and Risk

...the artist who has attained some degree
of proficiency in manipulation as taught
by this work, may by taxing his wits a little,
devise no end of tricks for himself, with
the advantage that they will not be "shop
worn" articles.

S. W. ERDNASE

O UR FOCUS SO FAR HAS BEEN to demystify the
process of creative problem solving, to show
that Advantage Play executives can manufacture effective solutions in an efficient manner if they adopt a
systematic approach, challenge assumptions, draw on a
network of support, and *use their heads*. Most executives, however, believe that they must do more than just
solve problems. First, let's look at technology, which is
constantly changing. Many executives suffer from "technology anxiety," the fear of not coping with or
capitalizing on the opportunity that technology presents.
How does technology factor into The Mechanics of
Problem Solving? Second, many executives have a secret
if not an expressed desire to be innovative. They compare themselves to others and are afraid that they fall
short of the mark. How does The Mechanics of Problem
Solving help an executive become an innovative player

in the marketplace? Third, what about the risk factor? Many executives know what has to be done to solve a problem but worry about the risks involved in implementing the solution. This chapter will address these concerns from the perspective of Advantage Play.

Although you may not be aware of it, magicians have always had a keen interest in technology and the application of technology to their craft. There have been some interesting by-products. The movies, for example, owe a huge debt to magicians. Magicians like George Melies and David Devant were pioneers in film production, exhibition, and distribution, and almost every major film comedian, from Buster Keaton and Charles Chaplin to Steve Martin and Woody Allen, have been amateur magicians.

Many regard technology as a form of magic. Indeed, Arthur C. Clarke wrote, "Any advanced technology is indistinguishable from magic." Most interpret this to mean that advanced technology is anything that looks like magic. In other words, if the audience believes that it looks magical—without explanation—it is advanced technology. Although this may be true from the perspective of the audience, it is certainly not true from the perspective of the Advantage Player. Advantage Play executives know that there is no such thing as magic. Technology is a tool, the same as any other sleight in the repertoire one can employ to achieve a magical effect.

Jean Eugène Robert-Houdin is considered the father of modern magic. A true innovator, Robert-Houdin had gained acclaim in Paris in the 1840s with his private salon of magic. He discarded the trappings of the profession, wore sophisticated evening attire instead of flowing robes, and—unbeknownst to his public—coupled scientific principles with his ability in sleight of hand to create absolute miracles. In 1860, Napoleon III enlisted Robert-Houdin to travel to Africa and demonstrate to the superstitious the superiority of European magic. To accomplish this diplomatic agenda, Robert-Houdin performed *The Light and Heavy Chest.*

In effect, he invited the strongest member of the rebellious tribe onto his stage and stated that he could take away that person's strength with just a wave of his wand. To prove his assertion, Robert-Houdin asked the strong man to lift the small chest that had been placed there. The participant did so with little effort. Robert-Houdin waved his wand towards the man and then motioned for him to try and lift the case again. Try as he might the native could not lift the small case from the floor. His strength had vanished. A second wave of the wand caused the subject to flee from the theater in pain. The secret, of course, was science and showmanship. Robert-Houdin was a pioneer with electricity. He created a chest that could apparently be both light and heavy by constructing and concealing an electromagnet beneath the stage and lining the chest with metal. After the wave of his wand, Robert-Houdin's offstage assistant would throw the secret switch creating the electromagnetic field. When the native reached the point of exhaustion, the voltage was increased sending electric shocks through the handle. The native ran from the theater in pain. From the point of view of the tribesmen, *The Light and Heavy Chest* was magic. For Robert-Houdin, the technology of electromagnetism was just another tool he could employ to achieve his client's objective.

The Advantage Player, too, regards technology as something that can be manipulated to achieve a desired objective. Technology is a tool, not an effect. Advantage Players know that as soon as you regard technology as something magical, you have become a spectator, not an innovator. Technology can be seductive. We can become so enamored by its sophistication and beauty that we let the technology become *the effect.* We let the tail wag the dog. Remember the words of Michelangelo: "Sometimes the means of expression can become so exquisite that the effect is lost." Advantage Players ask what technology does, not how it works.

Today's business climate emphasizes innovation. Executives believe that innovation provides them with a competitive advantage in the marketplace. Just as many rush into problem solving without having really determined the objective, many want to be innovative and yet do not understand the meaning of innovation. Tell me, would you consider a tea kettle that could answer intelligently and in a human voice questions put to it by a spectator when the latter placed its spout to his or her ear as something innovative? Probably not. Inanimate objects speak to us all the time. Many of us have children who use walkie-talkies to communicate with each other throughout the house. No big deal. It certainly was, however, in 1907.

In 1907, a wealthy amateur magician, spirit detective, and loan shark in Omaha, Nebraska, named David P. Abbott created a *talking tea kettle*—a tea kettle that would answer intelligently and in a human voice questions put to it by a spectator when the spout was placed to the ear. The secret depended on the wireless induction microphone principle discovered in 1885 by Thomas Edison. Abbott used magic to mask the use of this new technology. He concealed an induction coil around the sides of a papier-mâché kettle. This induction coil did double-duty as a diaphragm-speaker. The illusion was activated by electromagnetic induction and operated by an off-stage female assistant who listened in to questions with a microphone concealed in the performance room and who answered the questions over a speaker system that activated the kettle's induction coil. This was certainly innovative in 1907. The concept and sound of wireless communication was foreign to the ears of his audience. His audience believed that a spirit inhabited the tea kettle. No other explanation was possible. It caused a sensation.

Whether or not something is innovative depends on your point of view. Hence, there are four forms of innovation:

- Something is innovative if you have never seen it;
- Something is innovative if your staff, clients, or customers have never seen it;
- Something is innovative if your competition has never seen it; and
- Something is innovative if the world at large has never seen it.

These four forms of innovation are incremental in difficulty. It is much easier to discover things that are new to you and new to your constituency than it is to discover things that your competition or the world at large has never seen. Achieving either of the latter two is like winning the World Series by hitting a home run in the bottom of the ninth inning in the seventh and final game. It has been done but once. These are not great statistics on which to build a business plan. Finding out things that are new to you and new to your customers, however, is within the realm of achievement for the Advantage Player. It doesn't matter how old the trick may be. The first question should always be: "Does it solve the problem?" Whether or not people are familiar with the technology should be secondary to whether or not the technology delivers the solution. Advantage Play executives focus on application, not novelty. It is much easier to discover new applications for existing principles than it is to discover new principles that solve new problems.

I often design interactive promotions and displays for trade shows. Statistics show that after the product demonstrations—think kitchen knives—magic is the most effective way of drawing attention to a product or service in a trade show environment. One of my clients was a cellular phone company. The company's objective was to entertain and inform potential customers at a trade show presentation. I designed a mindreading cellular phone to achieve this objective. Someone would merely look at a card in a deck of cards and then be handed a cellular phone. The participant would then dial the psychic hot line and be guided through the system by a voice messaging service.

"Thank you for making the psychic cellular connection. If you are thinking of a black card, press one. If you are thinking of a red card, press two. If you are thinking of a court card—one with a picture on it—press three." The participant would press the appropriate number on the telephone keypad. The messaging system would continue. "You are thinking of a red card...it is a two... it is the two of hearts!" The look on the faces of the participants was worth the price of admission.

Here's the secret. I employed the principle of the cyclical stack used in *The Tossed Out Deck*. In this case I used a deck that consisted of just three cards—the king of hearts, the ten of spades, and the two of hearts. I placed the ace of spades on the bottom of the deck to block the first card in the cyclical stack from view. I placed an elastic band around the deck to secure the stack during the course of the presentation. Applying the principle of *The Tossed Out Deck*, the participant was forced to look at one of the three force cards. Once the spectator had glimpsed a card, the deck was put away— switched for a regular deck in my pocket—and the spectator given the "mindreading" cellular phone. The mindreader cellular phone, of course, was nothing more than an ordinary cellular phone. The psychic hot line was simply the voice messaging service at my home. I simply altered the answering machine message attached to each voice-mail box. Each message revealed the identity of one of the three force cards. I enjoy performing this effect at high-tech and computer trade shows because the audience assumes that the technology is much more sophisticated than it really is. Some believe, for example, that the cellular phone has a voice-recognition computer chip embedded in it that could process the necessary information. Never underestimate the power of the imagination.

I have applied the principle of *The Tossed Out Deck* to other presentations. Imagine a mindreading computer system. That's right. Five people think of playing cards and the computer generates graphic images of the mental selections. Easy to accomplish once you know how. The images of five cards, the five cards that correspond to the cards in the cyclical stack of *The Tossed Out Deck*, are scanned and pasted into a PowerPoint™ presentation. The images are set to advance on a timer. The deck is displayed, wrapped up with the elastic band and tossed into the audience. Five people are selected to open the pack and take a peek at a playing card. Once the pack has been returned, the mindreading notebook computer is introduced and the PowerPoint™ presentation advanced. The first slide in the presentation instructs everyone who selected a card to stand. The next slide instructs each person to think of his or her card. The third slide states, "Good…keep thinking…I'm getting a variety of images." The images of the five force cards appear and disappear before their eyes. The final slide states, "If I projected the image of the card you had in your mind, please sit down."

Another client presented a different problem. The company had developed an operating system for computers that could work across platforms and applications. The company's objective was to move a crowd from the perimeter of a trade show booth to the interior to witness a product demonstration. Once again, I applied the principle of *The Tossed Out Deck*. I explained to the audience that the deck of cards represented many different programs on a system and that they represented different users on different platforms in that system. I had five people open the deck and note the name of a card. I continued by explaining that a mindreading computer system that used a unique operating system to translate thoughts into a common language and then project these thoughts onto a large screen was located inside the theater. In order for the computer to project these thoughts, however, it must distinguish those who are thinking of a card from those who are not. I stated, "If you are thinking of a card, please come into the theater and *stand* in front of a chair. If you are not thinking of a card, please come into the theater and *sit* in a chair. Come!" The attendees shuffled into the theater. The computer presentation started and eventually projected the names of the five force cards onto the screen. Once again the five participants, each of whom had glimpsed a card, sat down after the computer had projected the five images. Not only was the audience entertained but I had accomplished my client's primary objective: moving a large number of people into a theatrical setting to see a more sophisticated and targeted corporate presentation.

Many companies advocate *thinking outside the box*. Edward de Bono and his pioneering work on lateral thinking inspired this term. The nine-dot puzzle is not only a good visual metaphor for lateral thinking but it also illustrates how something old can be something new to the uninitiated. I assumed that de Bono invented this puzzle—a claim that he never actually makes. I discovered years later that this puzzle, which has spawned a worldwide following of so-called *outside-the-box* thinkers, was published as early as 1903 by Ellis Stanyon in his periodical *Magic*. A puzzle expert has since informed me that the nine-dot puzzle dates back much further, at least to the 1850s, and is actually based on a business management case study of how tree planters can plant trees equidistantly apart in the most efficient manner. The puzzle as a visual metaphor for lateral thinking is innovative if you have never seen it.

Advantage Play executives know not just *how* things work but also *why* they work. It is only by knowing *why* something works that one can discover new applications—innovative applications—for those principles. Corning Glass, for example, has had the ability to manufacture non-glare glass for decades. But non-glare glass was not a tremendous seller. Recently, however, the company has discovered a new application for the technology—the use of non-glare glass in flat-screen computer monitors—and sales have skyrocketed. Advantage Play executives study their work and continually look for new applications.

As mentioned earlier, many executives are concerned with risk, particularly where technology is involved. Risk is what separates real life from illusion. Although risk can be reduced, it can never be eliminated. Many an Advantage Player has orchestrated the deal only to discover that chance has dealt someone else a stronger hand. Advantage Players can only orchestrate the *advantage*. There is no guarantee that they will win every time. Like a casino that has a statistical advantage in a game of chance, Advantage Players win in the long term. How then, do Advantage Play executives manage risk?

First, Advantage Players understand the nature of risk. They understand that *real risk* is different from *perceived risk*. One reason that Harry Houdini is an icon of the twentieth century is because the public believes—

perceives—that he did extraordinarily *risky* escapes. One of Houdini's most celebrated feats, for example, involved being submerged in a large milk can. The milk can, of course, had been inspected by members of the audience prior to the performance and the audience had also witnessed bucket after bucket of water being poured into the can. Houdini would explain the difficulty—the impossibility—of what he was about to do. He would then enter the can. Water, displaced by his weight, would gush from the can to the stage. Finally, just before he was totally submerged in the can and water was added to the top and the lid secured by padlocks, Houdini would ask the audience to hold its breath. This simple request was a brilliant piece of showmanship because it made each individual acutely aware of the danger. Once Houdini was totally submerged and the lid secured, a curtain was drawn around the cabinet. After what seemed an eternity—with each audience member well out of breath—Houdini, "exhausted," would stagger through the curtains. The curtains were opened and the milk can was intact. There was no trace of how he possibly could have escaped.

Although the perception of danger was great, in reality the danger was just an illusion. Houdini could escape from the milk can in seconds. Once out of the can, he would stand behind the curtain and wait. Legend has it that he would sometimes pass the time reading a newspaper hidden in the cabinet. He would wait for the moment when the tension was so great that the only way the audience could release it was to applaud madly. At that point in time, and not a second before, Houdini would put the newspaper away and stagger through the curtains to tumultuous applause. Houdini was the master at creating the expectation of risk where none existed.

One of the reasons it is difficult to separate real risk from perceived risk is because most of us spend our time pretending that our work is harder than it really is. We forget that we are just like Houdini, wanting to make the simplest task appear to be difficult. People are remunerated on the basis of how difficult their work appears to be rather than how difficult it really is. Reputation and reward are reserved for people who perform tasks that others perceive to be difficult. To reduce the stress associated with risk, however, the Advantage Play executive must distinguish the perception of risk from the reality of risk and then take measures to reduce the real risk.

Now, you already know how to manage risk. The principles of Advantage Play apply. The Mechanics of Problem Solving help to reduce risk. Have you defined the objective? Have you challenged assumptions? Have you drawn on your Creative Infrastructure to generate multiple options? Have you explored those multiple options so that you can be truly responsive to adverse market conditions? Have you evaluated the feasibility of the options based on your inventory of experience and the inventory of experience of the people you work with and admire? Have you put together a game plan for implementing the solution? Have you worked at trying to implement it? If you have done all of this, you will have minimized the risk.

Finally, Advantage Players minimize risk by exercising control—dictating the manner in which the decisions are made and implemented. Fortunately, most people are all too willing to relinquish control. When my client wanted to move people from the perimeter of the trade show booth to the interior and I said, "Come!" people walked into the theater. They followed my lead. You either lead or you follow. There is no in-between. Even when events appear to be beyond control, the Advantage Player is doing everything within his or her power to maintain control and minimize risk.

Several years ago I was speaking at a conference for revenue authorities—the people who police our tax system. Much of my presentation focused on themes I have set out in this book. I was explaining Advantage Play. Two members of the group stood up. They declared that they themselves played poker on a regular basis and there was no way I could possibly win if they dealt the cards. Needless to say, I accepted the challenge. I shoved the four aces that were face up on the table back into the deck and handed the pack to them. They shuffled the cards thoroughly but before that they sent me out of the room. Once I was ushered back into the room, I asked them to indicate which hand was mine. I picked it up, turned it over. I had the four aces!

Now, I only accepted the challenge because I knew that I could still be in control even if the deck was shuffled and dealt by another person. How? The aces were never in the pack. While it may have appeared as though I shoved the aces back into the deck, in reality I performed a sleight, S. W. Erdnase's *Diagonal Palm Shift*, that deposited the aces surreptitiously into my left hand. I just took the aces with me when I left the room. I told the others, however, to make sure that the duo did not cheat. The cards had to be shuffled and dealt fairly. They were not to look at the cards before they were

dealt. This was a reasonable request in light of the oner-
ous conditions that were imposed on me. My objective,
however, was to focus attention on the deal rather than
how many cards were left in the deck.

When I returned and everyone picked up their
respective cards, I simply switched four cards from my
poker hand for the four aces that I had concealed. I
turned over my hand after everyone else showed their
hands. They were so knocked out that it was child's
play to add the four indifferent cards back to the pack.
Now, I could do all of this because I had done it many
times before. Even though it appeared to the audience
that I had lost control, I still retained it. I just didn't let
them in on the secret.

If you review the magic I have presented throughout this work, you will discover that each routine
requires the performer to manage the spectator. Each
routine requires the performer to create the illusion that
the spectator has free will; that his or her actions determine cause and effect. The end result is always the
same. Risk is reduced so that the Advantage Player can
achieve the objective.

A D V A N T A G E P L A Y

1. Technology is not magic. Technology is a tool that one uses to achieve a magical effect.
2. Do not become so enamored of the sophistication of the technology that you let the technology become the effect.
3. Innovation depends on the point of view of the audience. Something is innovative if you, your customers, the competition, or the world has never seen it.
4. Seek incremental forms of innovation—things new to you and new to the customers whose problems you are trying to solve.
5. Advantage Players focus on application, not novelty. It is easier to discover new applications for existing principles than it is to discover new principles for existing problems.
6. Risk is what separates real life from illusion. It is inherent in Advantage Play.
7. Differentiate between *real risk* and *perceived risk.*
8. Minimize real risk with The Mechanics of Problem Solving.
9. You either lead or follow. There is no in-between. Advantage Players lead.

CHAPTER SEVEN

Advantage Sales

...the professional player must never slop over. One single display of dexterity and his usefulness is past in that particular company, and the reputation is liable to precede him in many other.

S. W. ERDNASE

A^{S THE CAB LEFT THE CURB,} the driver turned to me and asked, "So did you see that show last night?" "Copperfield?" I replied. "Yeah, that one," the driver responded. The driver was picking me up from the airport and must have surmised from my baggage that I was a magician and as a television special by David Copperfield had aired the night before, he obviously had some questions. The driver continued, "That trick, did it work for you?" I asked, "The trick with the cards?" imagining that he was referring to a piece of magic that Copperfield performed in which each viewer participated at home with his or her own cards. In effect, Copperfield divined the location of a card each spectator had in his or her mind. "Yeah, that one. Did it work for you?" "Yes," I replied. "Did you think of the queen of clubs?" he asked, the queen of clubs being the card that he had in his mind while interacting with the program. "No," I said, "I was thinking of the jack of hearts." "And it still worked?" he said with astonishment. I said, "Yes." He shook his head and muttered, "Amazing."

Now, this trick sounds impressive because you probably made the same mistake as the cab driver. Copperfield divined the *location* of the card, not its *identity*. The driver misremembered the effect and made the erroneous assumption that Copperfield addressed each individual viewer watching at home, naming the specific card he or she had in mind. The driver's misrepresentation is not an isolated occurrence. Most people who participated at home misremember *the effect*. It was designed that way. David Copperfield is the finest illusionist in the world today, not because his magic is particularly more astounding than other top tier performers, but because he knows that people remember *the effect* more than the methodology, and he makes sure that they remember the effect as he portrays it. He relies on *false memory*—people creating autobiographical references or memories of events that did not occur but that they recount and believe as being real based on the images he paints in their imagination.

David Copperfield can sell his *effects* better than his contemporaries. Success comes only to those who can sell. Every consumer has choice, not only of products and services, but also of ideas. If you want your ideas to be implemented—and who doesn't—you must sell your family, friends, colleagues, customers, or clients on the idea of using them. You have to sell your solutions. This chapter discusses *Advantage Sales*, the technique Advantage Players use to sell solutions and create false memories that build relationships and create additional sales.

Several years ago I was asked to address a group of management consultants at a weekend retreat. The theme for the retreat was the concept of *Strategic Selling* based on the sales system advocated by Stephen E. Heiman and Diane Sanchez in their best-selling book of the same name. The management consultants provided me with a copy of *Strategic Selling* to make sure that my message reinforced the approach suggested in the book. I read the book and, like most others, was very impressed. Not only was it *the real work* for my money, but also it dovetailed exceptionally well with everything that I advocate. The most refreshing thing about *Strategic Selling* is that it shuns the concept of manipulating people to close a sale.

Anyone can make a sale and although sales may contribute to the short-term health of an organization, they are not responsible for the longevity of the organization. Organizations prosper because of the relationships they build with their customers, relationships based on solving problems rather than the sale of a particular product or service. People hate being manipulated and, although a sale may result, the distaste for the process will terminate or temper the relationship. Also, *selling* requires more than just taking an order for a product or service. The sales clerk at the haberdashery who produces the shirt of the appropriate size and color pursuant to a customer's request hasn't *sold* anything. All he has done is take an order. Advantage Sales is much more proactive.

Advantage Sales creates wealth by selling products or services that solve problems. Advantage Players have no interest in selling something just for the sake of making a sale. The only sales that they are interested in making are the ones that solve the problem. Advantage Sales are *win-win* scenarios. Advantage Players use The

Mechanics of Problem Solving as a framework for selling solutions. It is a strategic approach to problem solving. The suggestions I have made to make you more efficient problem solvers within each stage of The Mechanics of Problem Solving are tactics that Advantage Players also employ to become more effective salespeople.

The first stage in The Mechanics of Problem Solving is like the first step in *Strategic Selling*: understand who your customers are and what is the problem they need to solve. The authors of *Strategic Selling* caution the reader to challenge the assumption of who the real decision maker is in the buying process. The authors cite many examples of salespeople who assume that the money is in the bank, so to speak, because of a personal connection the salesperson may have with the buyer when, in fact, the real decision maker was someone else outside that circle or relationship. Advantage Players understand the importance of defining the objective, a large part of which is making sure that you know who, in fact, is the decision maker.

Part of defining the objective is also articulating the resources, such as time, money, and personnel, that must be factored into any solution. The last thing you want to hear partway through the implementation process is that the resources are not available. Advantage Players rarely encounter this problem if the specific allocation of resources is recognized as an integral part of the client's objective at the beginning of the sales process. Clients often forget to stipulate these conditions. The client must be reminded and provide instruction. Clients rarely focus on or understand two things at once. Each *effect* or objective must be broken down into simple tasks if it is to be communicated effectively. Breaking the objective down into a series of simple tasks serves a primary role in Advantage Sales. Not only will decision makers understand that their objectives will be met but they will also be able to communicate this fact to others within the client organization. If the answer is "no" at any point in this stage of the process, you have either made an error as to the ultimate objective or have failed to set up an appropriate line of communication in which the decision maker could inform you that the objective has changed.

Stages two and three of The Mechanics of Problem Solving also facilitate Advantage Sales. People want to make informed decisions before they buy. Buying ideas is no exception. One way to make sure the customer is comfortable with the purchasing decision is to show her that you have created a Multiple Option Universe. If you do not convince clients that they have multiple options, they will be forced to conduct their own investigation to see if other options exist. This is the time to explain how you arrived at your solution. You have evaluated the options based on your inventory of experience and the inventory of experience housed in your Creative Infrastructure. Your ability to determine *the* solution rather than *a* solution separates the winners from the losers. Many people can define objectives and generate solutions. The trick is to pick the right solution. Once the client assents to your evaluation, it is time to close the sale. The client must sign off on the steps and the resources that are required to implement the solution. If the client objects to any of the above, you must be prepared to defend your methodology and your choices. If you have really done your work, it will take a great deal of thought on the part of the client to object in a reasonable manner to what you have proposed.

The significance of Advantage Sales became apparent to me when I was approached by an association of law office managers. The managers had a business problem that was easy to describe. The lawyers for whom they worked often refused to authorize any initiative suggested by someone other than another lawyer. In one sense, lawyers are the most difficult customers one can encounter because they are trained to think negatively. That is, they have to identify everything that can go wrong with a transaction in order to suggest an appropriate course of action for their own clients. Lawyers believe that it is no good identifying ten things that can go wrong when in reality twelve exist, because it will be the two that they have failed to identify that will torpedo the strategy.

Lawyers are also the ultimate consumers because they are trained to challenge assumptions and to conduct due diligence. Due diligence means not taking someone's word as being *the truth*. If a client is going to buy a factory, the lawyer sends someone out to make sure the factory physically exists. The managers had a difficult time persuading the lawyers to adopt a particular course of action because the lawyers were skeptical inquirers—thinking negatively, challenging assumptions, and conducting their own due diligence.

Most salespeople in this situation would find fault with the customer. Advantage Sales, however, suggests that the fault lies with the salesperson. The managers could not get their ideas implemented because they did not take the time to sell their customers—the lawyers—

on the merits of their ideas. They just assumed that because they had been hired to perform a task, their instructions would be implemented. The managers forgot a fundamental principle. Contrary to popular belief, lawyers do not instruct their clients; lawyers advise their clients. The client must decide whether to accept or reject the advice. It is an important distinction. The client must always be comfortable with the solution. The same principle applies in selling solutions. You cannot expect someone with little expertise in an area to understand fully the significance of ideas that are in essence developed in camera—that is to say, behind closed doors or in a situation where the end beneficiary is not privy to the process. This principle applies regardless of what product, service, or solution one is selling. Advantage Players recognize that to sell solutions, they must bring the client up to speed with not only the process but with the decisions that were made along the way. The client must be sold on the merits of the idea.

I suggested to the managers that if the lawyers *signed off* at each stage of the problem-solving sequence, the lawyers themselves would recognize the merits of the plan and feel comfortable that all the issues had been recognized, examined, and accounted for, and that, based on the assumptions that had been made, the solution they had submitted would be the one that was implemented. As the relationship between the lawyers and the managers developed, there was less need to present the information in such a mechanical approach. The relationship between the problem solver and the client developed to the point where the client knew that the problem will be solved and that it would not be necessary to monitor the process so thoroughly. After all, most people go to someone to solve their problems because they themselves do not have enough time to do so in the first place. Although a client may state that he or she is interested in how a particular problem is solved—particularly after the fact—they are probably just being polite. Clients just want to know that the problem is solved. As a creative problem solver, you must be prepared to explain the mechanics of your approach and why it will deliver the right solution.

Advantage Sales is more than just selling solutions. Advantage Sales is also about creating a reputation that attracts business. Advantage Players want people to talk about their work in a positive manner and, as you probably expect, the Advantage Player does not leave this to chance. Solving a problem in a creative manner is no guarantee that the customer will express her enthusiasm for your work to others. Fortunately, there is a technique that ensures you get more than the praise you deserve. Underutilized by most, this technique of Advantage Sales *adds value* to the relationship to such an extent that customers are so satisfied they go away and tell other people what happened. The technique is quite simple. You must plant the seed so the customer misremembers what took place. In other words, the greatest way to add value in any relationship is for the client to focus on *the effect* rather than *the methodology* and forget what actually happened.

Few clients remember the specifics of what was done for them. It is like attending a rock concert. Bruce Springsteen may knock your socks off for two hours singing hit after hit. Most in attendance, however, will describe the experience simply as *awesome*. By the same token, you could deliver the most fantastic solution imaginable but few clients will be able to describe shortly thereafter the specifics in any significant detail. Although magic is an art that relies on deception, I am not suggesting that you deceive your clients. On the contrary, I am merely suggesting that you think like an Advantage Player and recognize the lasting power of the final impression you leave with your clients. Clients remember the final image, thought, suggestion, or action and not the fact that you spent an incredible amount of time and energy defining objectives, challenging assumptions, creating a Multiple Option Universe, evaluating options based on inventories of experience and Creative Infrastructures, and implementing the solution. You will work very hard to deliver the solution. To increase sales you also must work very hard at developing subtle ways for the client to remember what you want them to remember. Take stock of the images you create in the mind of the person whose problem you solve. Again, perception is reality. Determine what you can do to improve that perception. Avoid, however, the quick fix. Advantage Players recognize that relationships are built on the cumulative effect of hundreds of apparently inconsequential details, not on a solitary gesture.

All of this, of course, is easier said than done. There is, however, one way to demonstrate these techniques in a controlled environment and monitor the effect of people misremembering detail. As an illustration, let me introduce you to Dai Vernon's *The Trick That Cannot Be Explained*. No ordinary pseudo-psychic experiment, *The Trick That Cannot Be Explained* requires the performer to set out the objective, develop a Multiple Option Universe, exercise great editorial judgment based on his or her inventory of experience, follow an implementation strategy, and yet be flexible enough to alter the tactics based on the conditions that arise during the course of the performance. Most important, the performer must sow the seeds so that each audience member not only goes away from the performance exclaiming that he or she witnessed a miracle, but also so that the person feels compelled to tell others what happened in much more powerful and thought-provoking terms than anything that actually transpired.

THE TRICK THAT CANNOT BE EXPLAINED

The performer makes a prediction about a particular card in the deck. The spectator is not privy to the prediction. The prediction is tabled before the trick is started. The spectator shuffles the pack. The spectator selects a card. The performer opens the prediction to show that he or she correctly predicted the selected card.

While it was relatively easy to describe *the effect*, it is much more difficult to describe the methodology. The secret, in essence, is that after the performer has made a secret prediction of a card in the deck—any card—he makes the spectator select that card in an apparently free and fair manner. The performer concludes *the effect* making it appear that whatever actions the spectator performed in selecting the card is by design. In reality,

the performer improvised the entire procedure,
responding to the actions and information the spectator unknowingly transmitted to the performer as
the spectator handled the cards. Now, let me break
it down into more manageable segments.

There are four stages to the trick. First, the
performer must make a prediction. Second, the
spectator must shuffle the cards. Third, unknowingly the spectator must select the predicted card.
Fourth, the performer must construct the story of
the effect and plant it in the mind of the spectator
so that he misremembers what actually took
place. Each stage has its nuances. We will discuss
several of them. It is impossible to canvas them
all. Remember, this *is* the trick that cannot be
explained. Let's start with the prediction.

First, you can predict any card that you desire.
There are no restrictions. You will make the prediction and the spectator will select the predicted
card. *Advantages that are bound to ultimately
give a percentage in favor of the professional are
absolutely essential to his existence.* We should
use the opportunity of making the prediction to
create whatever advantages we can that will assist
us in achieving our objective. For example, some
people naturally gravitate toward certain playing
cards. It is not uncommon for a woman, when
asked spontaneously to name a particular card, to
say the queen of hearts. Dai Vernon always tried
to size up the person assisting and predict a card
the spectator might point out in the pack. He
found, for example, that shrewd card players

often try to outwit the performer by nearly always pointing to a small card, one with a low face value. Again, the success or failure of the trick does not depend on the name of the card that you predict. One only seeks advantages. Once the performer has a card in mind, he must make the prediction. A simple way to do this is to write the name of the card on a piece of paper or on the back of a business card. The prediction is tabled face down before the spectator. We are now ready for Stage Two.

The spectator is requested to pick up the pack and shuffle it. The performer must create the impression that the spectator is in control of the entire procedure. This, of course, is completely false because the spectator will follow the performer's arcane instructions. Remember *Virtual Participation.*

Also note you will be thinking on your feet. You must control the timing and flow of the presentation in order to give yourself that extra time to analyze the situation and develop appropriate tactics. Thus, your vocal delivery and physical actions should be at a casual and leisurely pace.

Once the spectator has shuffled the cards, you must force the spectator to select the card that matches your prediction. The only way to do this effectively is to draw on one of the various options you have created in a Multiple Option Universe. Although improvisation is required, you will be applying one or several tactics to achieve your objective within a strategy that was clearly formed, articulated and practiced in advance. *The Trick That Cannot Be Explained* is a combination of strategy and tactics. Let's look at some of the options available to us in Stage Three.

First, as the spectator shuffles the cards, he may inadvertently flash, that is accidentally reveal to you, the identity of one or two cards in the pack. You may, for example, secretly learn the identity of the top or bottom cards in the pack. You will also be able to note whether or not those cards stay in the same positions after the shuffle. If one of those cards matches the card that you predicted, instruct the spectator to turn over either the top card or the deck itself, if revealing the bottom card, and stop. If you cannot secretly see the identity of a particular card or if there is no match, continue with the presentation by asking the spectator to place the deck face up on the table.

If the card that matches your prediction is staring you in the face, stop the selection procedure. If not, ask the spectator to cut the deck. The spectator may actually cut to the card you have predicted. If not, ask him to complete the cut and cut the deck once more thereby giving you a second chance with the same ruse. Through skillful management you have created at least three opportunities for the spectator to cut to the predicted card and yet from the spectator's point of view, the trick is just beginning.

As soon as you realized that he did not cut the predicted card to the face of the pack, spread the cards openly out in a line taking time to make sure that each and every card is visible. You can ask the spectator whether he is satisfied that the cards are truly in a random position. Determine the location of the predicted card in the spread and consider what options are available to force it on the spectator.

If at a prime position, that is anywhere near either end of the pack, note the number of cards that separate it from the end. Is it the second, third, fourth, fifth, sixth, or seventh card, for example, from the end? If the card is near the end, you most likely will be able to spell to or count down, that is remove one card for each letter or number, to arrive at the predicted card. If, for example, you have ascertained that the predicted card is the eighth card from the top, and the top card is an eight, you are home free. Scoop up the cards and turn them face down in your left hand. Turn over the top card to show its value and then count down the requisite number of cards to arrive at the predicted card. Please note that you have a three-card margin of error. Again, if the predicted card is the eighth card from the top and the top card of the pack is an eight, simply show the top card, declare its value and count down eight cards making the indicator card—the eight—the first of the cards counted and dealt to the table. If the predicted card is the ninth card from the top and the top card of the pack is an eight, turn over the top card of the pack, declare its value and place it aside. Immediately count eight cards from the top of the deck into a pile on the table. The last card dealt—really the ninth card from the top of the pack—is the predicted card. If the predicted card is the tenth card from the top, turn over the eight, declare its value and place it aside. Immediately deal eight cards from the top into a pile on the table and stop. Turn over the top card of the remaining cards in the deck—really the tenth card from the top—and you arrive at the predicted card.

In addition to having a numerical value, each card possesses at least three names—a first name, a middle name, and a last name. The first name is the alphabetical spelling of the number or name, for example e-i-g-h-t or k-i-n-g. The middle name is always the same. It is o-f. The third name is always the suit, that is, h-e-a-r-t-s or whatever the suit may be. Thus, a jack of spades on top of the deck could be used to locate a card at a variety of positions. The performer could spell j-a-c-k, or j-a-c-k-s-p-a-d-e-s or j-a-c-k-o-f-s-p-a-d-e-s to arrive at the predicted card. Each variation in spelling also has a three-card margin of error.

What if, however, the predicted card resides near the center of the deck? Once again, many options are available to you. One option is to apply the technique of controlled elimination. Let's explore the application of this technique in more detail.

Remember that from the point of view of the participant, the trick is just beginning. The fact that the performer has made a prediction, the spectator has shuffled and cut the pack, and the cards have been spread out face up in a row on the table have all been preliminary actions or remarks. From the performer's point of view, he knows the location of the predicted card—somewhere near the center of the spread. The objective is to force the participant to select that card in the most direct manner possible.

Ask the spectator to raise his right or left hand, depending on the position of the spectator and the position of the predicted card. If the spectator is sitting across from you and the predicted card is slightly to the left of center, ask the spectator to use his left hand. If, however, the predicted card is to the right of center, ask the spectator to use his right hand and to hold that hand above the end of the spread. Ask the spectator to extend the index finger **(Photograph 7)** and then move the hand slowly in one direction above the cards. Watch the participant as he does this and caution him, if necessary, to move slowly and mysteriously. You must control the timing, as you will have to make several decisions. Instruct the spectator to place the finger on a card.

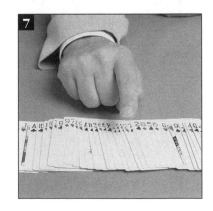

Sometimes the spectator will actually place his finger on the predicted card. If the participant touches the predicted card, ask him to remove it from the spread. You are set for the finish and can now proceed to Stage Four. If the spectator places the finger on a card adjacent to the predicted card, remove all the cards adjacent to the predicted card. You are left with the predicted card.

If the participant overshoots the predicted card, remove all the cards to the left or right of the card indicated, as the case may be, and ask him to repeat the process from the other side. He will probably overshoot the predicted card from the other side. Again, eliminate these cards from play. Pick up the remaining cards including the predicted card, re-spread the cards in a wider ribbon or arc on the table and repeat the elimination procedure. Don't forget, however, the other options that are available to you. The spectator may select at any time a card with a name or numeric value that will allow you to spell or count down to the predicted card.

Finally, here is one other sorting procedure that guarantees success. Assume that the predicted card is within five cards of an indicated card. Separate the five cards from the remainder of the pack and deal them face down onto the table. Place the other cards aside. Remind the spectator that you are eliminating cards. Ask the spectator to mix the cards on the table. He is to continue mixing until you snap your fingers, at which point he should turn over, that is turn face-up, three of the five cards. You must be prepared to make a rapid decision. If the spectator fails to turn over the predicted card, take the three face-up cards and place them with the other discards. You will then force the predicted card—one of the two cards remaining on the table—in a manner that I will describe in a few moments. If, however, the predicted card is one of the three selections, scoop up the two face-down cards and add them to the discards. Without hesitation, turn the three face-up cards back down and ask the spectator to mix them once again. Instruct the participant to turn over two cards at the sound of the snap. Once again, two options exist. If the spectator turns over two indifferent cards, remove them from play as you are left with the selection. If, however, he turns over the predicted card as one of the two, immediately pick up both cards and hand them to the participant. (You will apply this same technique if in the initial turnover the predicted card was one of the two cards left on the table.) Instruct the spectator to mix the two cards and then hold one in each hand. Remove the card remaining on the table. Ask the spectator to give you at the snap of your fingers one of the two cards he has in hand. He will hand you either the predicted card or the indifferent card. Regardless of which card you hold, ask the spectator if he would like to change his mind. This creates the illusion of free choice. If, in the end, you are holding the predicted card, hold it high and take the other card from the spectator and add it to the discards. If the participant is holding the predicted card, place the indifferent card handed to you with the discards. You are now ready for Stage Four. You must conclude the routine so that it registers in the spectator's imagination.

The power of the effect depends directly on the seeds you sow. Although your summation will vary depending on the course of action you employed to force the selection, you must emphasize *the effect.* *"You may recall that I made a prediction on this piece of paper while you were shuffling the cards. You shuffled and cut them to your heart's content.*

You arrived (cut to, pointed to, indicated, selected) one card. Isn't it strange how I was able to predict in advance the card that you have selected." Keep it simple and straightforward. Focus on the impossible and leave the spectator with a simple thought to repeat to others. Show the match. **(Photograph 8)**

We have only scratched the surface of *The Trick That Cannot Be Explained.* As you can see, there are many ways to achieve your objective. You will discover many other options and develop your favorites each time you experiment with *the effect.* Do not rush either the effect or the methodology. *The Trick That Cannot Be Explained* is a management exercise. You must manage how *the effect* unfolds, the methodology used to achieve your objective, and the image or impression that the spectator remembers. Inexperience makes one rush. Again, confidence comes from practice. Remember, avoid the temptation to conclude the effect with the first option that springs to mind. Patience is required. You are in control. The authors of *Strategic Selling* note the importance of *setting a strategy*, "that is doing whatever you have to do to put yourself in the best position to accomplish a particular objective or set of objectives." *The Trick That Cannot Be Explained* is an opportunity to perfect the practice of determining the best option. Make sure that you listen to the members of your audience after each performance. They will tell you, without prompting, what they believe took place. The power of the imagination is evident in every attempt to describe or reconstruct the effect. Recognize the power of *false memory* and harness its potential.

Finally, *The Trick That Cannot Be Explained* requires more *sleight of mind* than sleight of hand, meaning that the success or failure of the trick hinges more on the performer's capacity for management rather than digital dexterity. The *effect* is virtually impossible to reconstruct, even on subsequent viewings, because the procedure involved will most likely vary each time the trick is performed. In short, *The Trick That Cannot Be Explained* utilizes every technique that we have explored in this work and is a practical exercise that will expand your capacity for management and your ability to sell and create a reputation.

ADVANTAGE PLAY

1. Every customer has choice, not only of products and services but also of ideas. To be successful, you must sell your solutions.

2. Relationships are created and nurtured on the sale of solutions rather than the sale of individual products or services. The sale must be a win-win scenario.

3. The Mechanics of Problem Solving provide the strategy and tactics for strategic selling.

4. Discover the objective, challenge assumptions, generate options, evaluate, and implement the solution for your client.

5. Be patient. Avoid the temptation to conclude the sale with the first option that springs to mind. It is often the second or third option that produces the commercial triumph.

6. The greatest way to add value to a transaction is for the client to misremember what actually took place. Clients rarely remember the details, only *the effect*. Recognize the power of *false memory* and harness its potential.

7. Excessive vanity does prove the undoing of many experts. Avoid the temptation to show off or risk of becoming a past master in your profession.

The Advantage Team

*Proficiency in target practice is not the
sole qualification of the trap shooter. Many
experts with the gun who can nonchalantly
ring up the bull's eye in a shooting gallery
could not hit the side of a barn in a duel.
The greater the emergency, or the greater
the stakes, the greater the nerve required.*

S. W. ERDNASE

L AS VEGAS, NEVADA, IS A MAGNET for business. It has
become one of the major trade show centers in
North America and more and more companies are staging their annual sales conferences and corporate retreats
in this casino environment. Why is that? Perhaps it is
because casinos are, at least in North America, the last
cultural remnants of the Wild West, places that cater to
our sense of adventure and our secret desire to tempt
fate, but in a safe and secure environment. Most visitors
to Las Vegas fantasize about walking out of casinos as
millionaires. The Advantage Play executive cannot
afford to fantasize. He must deliver the effective solution
in his own casino environment—the world of business—each and every time.

Casino play accommodates a myriad of strategy and
tactics, all of which have their counterpart in the world

of business. When I ask participants in my workshops on creative problem solving how one can maximize the return on investment in casino play, the answers vary. Some suggest counting cards—tracking the value of cards that have been played in order to develop a better understanding of which cards remain in the deck and the probability of receiving them. Card counting is a conservative approach. Expert card counters can perhaps tip the odds so that they are even with or slightly better than that of the casino, not a great margin of profit for the work involved, particularly if you want to make a good living. Others advocate a more aggressive strategy: use sleight of hand to produce the winning hand. But as everyone knows, casinos have elaborate security systems that monitor all aspects of play, people, and the environment to thwart such tactics. All of the suggestions ignore one very important concept that we have only touched upon, a concept that helps the Advantage Player when the emergency is great and the stakes are high. The concept is teamwork.

You may recall that the cardsharp who profited at the Oxbridge Club in Chapter 1 did not work alone. He was assisted by the *mechanic*, the nimble fingered secret accomplice who placed the winning cards in his hand. There was also a third. The third member, known as the *cool out operator*, had the most difficult task. His job was to insure that *the money* stayed at the table. He had to convince the losers that their luck would change if they continued to play. He had to know, however, when to ease the money from the table so that it would return to play another day. The cool out operator managed the money on behalf of his teammates as if he were managing the return on investment of individual stocks in an investment portfolio. The members of the Oxbridge Club never had a chance because they played as individuals. Individuals can never beat a team.

The premier text on profiting in a casino through Advantage Play is *Cheating at Blackjack and Advantage Play* by Dustin D. Marks—a clever pseudonym for an author who, for obvious reasons, would like to remain anonymous. It suggests a team of people is required to defraud a casino. The team consists of a casino dealer, the *switcher,* the *Big Player* and a large cast of extras, each of whom has a clearly defined role to play in the operation. In essence, the casino dealer permits the *switcher* to exchange decks in play for a similar number of decks stacked to deliver winning hands to the *Big Player.* The *Big Player* will place all of the bets on behalf of the team. The cast of extras will provide the cover so that the trio does not get caught.

A team can only reap the rewards of Advantage Play if management knows how to assemble and direct its activities. Advantage Teams fail for many reasons. The areas that are of most concern to the Advantage Player are preparation and planning, recruiting the right team members, ensuring that communication is clear between members particularly during transitions, and practicing and rehearsing the implementation of the strategy. Let's look at these areas of concern in more detail.

Successful teams follow a game plan that is simple in concept but filled with detail and nuance. The game plan for defrauding a casino is quite simple: exchange the decks in play for decks that are ordered to deliver winning hands while casino personnel and security are distracted from the play. The viability of this plan can only be developed through extensive preparation, analysis, planning, and perspiration. The Advantage Player must understand all the nuances of the proposal, anticipate where the danger lies, and make sure that he has the people and strategy in place to counter it. The Mechanics of Problem Solving are an excellent template for what must be done and who must do it. It breaks the objective down into a series of simple but manageable tasks, each of which must be attended to by team members if the plan is to succeed. Further, The Mechanics ensures that the plan is well formulated, that anything that can go wrong won't go wrong because it has been addressed prior to implementation, or multiple options have been generated that will deal with such contingencies should they arise. Multiple options provide team members with the confidence needed to perform under pressure.

Once the plan is in place and the various roles defined, the manager must recruit the personnel to perform the tasks. One can only appoint the right people to the team if the transaction is thoroughly understood in advance. Many teams fail to deliver solutions because management has not determined the skill set required for each position or because they assume that the personnel in place already have the requisite skills. Advantage Play executives take nothing for granted. They assess and assemble each cast carefully. Although the stakes may be high, there is never enough return to warrant duplication of skills and services. The *dealer,* the *switcher,* and the *Big Player,* for example, each have a separate skill and must be recruited to perform that skill.

Now, how does a blackjack team recruit a *dealer*? The answer: discreetly. The team looks for a *dealer* with the courage, discretion, and acumen to become a team player. Often the managers will establish a relationship with a potential candidate as soon as that candidate has entered the program that will teach him how to deal. Management scouts these schools and programs like a professional sports team sources athletes from college or the junior leagues. Eventually they find the ideal candidate. A relationship is formed and maintained with each prospective candidate. His or her career is then tracked after graduation from the program. As casinos are in constant need of qualified dealers—the turnover rate is high—the potential candidate will be placed in a casino before long.

The dealer may join the team for a variety of reasons. The primary reason, of course, is the money. Dealers are paid poorly. They derive a large portion of their income from "tokes," that is tips from patrons who either like the service or fare well at the table. Dealers see large amounts of money exchange hands, very little of which comes to them. The team will pay the dealer 35 percent of the proceeds simply to turn a blind eye when the exchange of decks occurs. As the proceeds can easily total $100,000 or more, the dealer will earn approximately $35,000 for three seconds of work, three seconds being the time it takes to exchange the decks. Other considerations may also factor into a dealer's decision to join the team. Most dealers are treated poorly and supervised by pit bosses not known for either their intellectual or interpersonal skills. Finally, there is the pressure. Expectations run high on both sides of the table. Some dealers want to retire from the profession but lack the means with which to do so. The team can provide those means.

The *switcher* and the *Big Player* also have special skills. The *switcher* is most often a *mechanic* with a high degree of digital dexterity and nerves of steel. The *Big Player* must look and act like a *high roller*, be articulate and also have the ability to withstand the spotlight; it doesn't take long for blackjack to become a spectator sport. Advantage Play executives must constantly be on the lookout for potential team members and understand what will motivate them to join the team and perform to their full potential.

The Advantage Team must do more than just recruit the right personnel to exchange decks in order to profit at the blackjack table. Each member must perform a task in an order and manner determined by team management. The team will only succeed if each team member understands the mechanics of what he or she must do and, more importantly, how each team member *gets in* and *gets out* of what it is that must be done. Advantage teams often succeed or fail on the basis of how well they execute the transitions. A communication breakdown at any point in the transaction could prove to be catastrophic. Let's look at the steps involved in exchanging the cards.

First, the table must be secured. Every player at the table must be a member of the team. That's right. Team members must occupy every seat. As each player can play multiple hands, it only takes four team members to *lock up* a seven game layout and three team members to lock up all positions in a six game layout. There are many techniques members can use to lock up the table. The most direct method is to get people to leave the table and replace them with team members. A critical comment directed towards another player or the presence of an offensive person is usually enough for regular casino patrons to jump to another table. The team prefers a subtle approach, however, and tries not to attract attention to team members or the table. Once in place, each team member will bet the table minimum and use conventional strategy for play until the *switcher* sits down at the table and executes the exchange with the dealer.

To reduce the risk involved in the exchange, the team uses *turners* to distract casino patrons, floor personnel, and overhead cameras—the *eyes in the sky*—at the time of the switch. Ordinarily five *turners* are assigned to different areas or zones around the table. Two are responsible for the area in front of the game, two pick up anyone wandering by who may be looking at the table, and one *turner* distracts the pit boss. As the exchange takes but seconds, a simple question directed toward the casual viewer or pit boss is all that may be necessary to shift attention away from the table.

The team takes the same approach with the video surveillance system. A team member may, for example, cultivate a friendship with a member of the surveillance team and call that person at work at the exact time the switch is about to take place to distract him from his job. Security personnel are easy to misdirect. Further, the people employed to watch the monitors are not well trained, have little experience dealing cards, are poorly paid, and are isolated from other staff. Further, watching a bank of black and white television monitors day in and day out is a mind numbing experience. Many relieve the tedious nature of the job during working hours by amusing themselves with other activities—particularly during the graveyard shift. A phone call may be a welcome relief. The team also recognizes that there are not enough personnel to monitor every game simultaneously. The Advantage Team takes comfort in the fact that very few games are actually recorded on tape. It would be a very expensive and cumbersome task to record and store month after month of around-the-clock videotape coverage of casino play.

The physical mechanics of the switch of the cards itself are simple. When the table is secure and the dealer must shuffle the cards, the *switcher* removes a corresponding number of decks programmed to win, *the cooler*, from a custom made interior sling or pocket and places them on the table. The dealer picks up the cooler and places it in *the shoe*, the device the casino uses to hold the cards on the table for the deal, while the *switcher* picks up the casino cards, places them in the interior pocket and leaves the table. Again, the physical act of exchanging decks takes a matter of seconds. The *Big Player* enters the picture as the *switcher* leaves the table.

As *Erdnase* suggests, the Advantage Player considers nothing too trivial that in any way contributes to his success. The Advantage Team adopts the same strategy. In order to leave nothing to chance, the team may sponsor a known card counter or *Fake Big Player* to initiate action at another table. The surveillance team is often instructed by a pit boss or supervisor to focus on a particular game. Casino security will focus the camera on this area of play, an area well away from the real theater of operation. By the time this occurs, the exchange will have occurred and the *Big Player* will be in place.

Once the exchange is complete, the *Big Player* will buy into the game with a substantial amount of money and request that the game be reserved exclusively for him or her, that is to say no other players be allowed at the table. It is within the rights of the *Big Player* to do so provided he or she has the money. The objective, of course, is to get the *Big Player* to play one-on-one against the dealer. With the game reserved and the *Big Player* knowing the order of the cards, he or she will bet large and win *almost* every hand. Winning every hand, after all, would be too perfect and create undue suspicion. The *Big Player* must be prepared not only to place the bets but also withstand the scrutiny that will increase proportionately with each bet. It will not take long before the pit boss will monitor the turn of every card once losses mount for the casino. He will try to discover the history of the *Big Player*, where the player is from, and where he or she is staying. Once again, unflinching audacity is required. Once the *Big Player* retires from the table, he or she must maintain the aura of the *Big Player*, and take time to cash out the chips and pick up the winnings. Every phase of the game plan is important. Teams succeed or fail based on their commitment to the entire process.

As an Advantage Play executive, you must make sure that your team has received the requisite direction. Just as the Advantage Player must sell the customer on the solution, the Advantage Team leader must brief team members on what is required and why. As the chance of a breakdown in communication grows with the size of the team, each objective or task must be clear and concise so that each team member knows exactly when and what he or she has to do. Often team members are so eager to demonstrate their skill and convince the leaders of their worth that they proceed to the implementation stage without the essential skills or preparation to perform the required task. Advantage Play executives take nothing for granted. They ensure that team members know what has to be done and that the players commit themselves to the entire process, not just a particular role or function.

Advantage Play executives also ensure that the team has practiced individual parts and rehearsed the entire procedure before attempting to implement it. The team must practice and rehearse the plan so that it can be performed as effortlessly as breathing. Insufficient practice and rehearsal are the Achilles' heel of the Advantage Player. Practice and rehearsal are two different things. Practice is concerned with mastering an individual technique such as the exchange of cards. Rehearsal is concerned with developing confidence in the entire process and, in particular, the timing of the process. Practice and rehearsal instill and inspire confidence. Ultimately confidence creates grace under pressure— the ability to delay in the face of adversity the performance of an action until the appropriate moment.

Advantage Players understand the importance of practicing and rehearsing in a real world environment. The team that plans on switching decks at the card table, for example, erects a practice area with a table that is the same height, width, and surface as the table in the casino. The *Big Player* will practice placing the appropriate bets by working with a dealer who actually turns the cards. He will also practice maintaining his ground and fielding questions from a pit boss. The team will brief the *Big Player* like a lawyer briefs his client before a trial to make sure that each response is appropriate in the circumstances. The team will then repeatedly rehearse the entire sequence, plus contingency plans, from start to finish. It is the only way to ensure success.

If all of this information about defrauding a casino is true, why is this strategy not more widely known? First, casinos are not likely to advertise anything that demonstrates vulnerability. More importantly, if everything goes according to plan, the casino will not know that they have been deceived. There will be, for example, no videotape record of the switch for review. Casinos are aware that statistically a high roller might have an extraordinary run of luck but it cannot predict with any degree of certainly when such luck will occur. All it can do is invite the high roller to return as the odds are such that in the long run, the high roller will lose everything he or she has won in the past plus some. Casinos track the winners for this reason and offer to fly them in, provide room, food and beverages, and other special services to keep them playing. Successful teams keep quiet so that they can continue to do business another day. No one wants to be, as S. W. Erdnase would say, a past master in the profession.

Now, you are probably thinking that if team members spent a fraction of the amount of their time and expertise in legitimate business, they would not have to resort to fraud and larceny to succeed. You're right but for whatever reason—the environment in which they were raised or the gene pool from which they emerge—they can't. You can.

You can assemble a team that leverages individual skills to accomplish objectives well beyond the reach of the lone player, a team that permits conservative individuals to adopt a more aggressive approach in problem solving but also tempers an aggressive strategy into a more conservative one, transforming real risk into perceived risk without diluting the rewards commensurate with the perception of difficulty. So, use the example of Advantage Play in a casino as a procedural checklist to improve the performance of your team. Ask: Have we done our homework? Have we challenged assumptions and developed multiple approaches to the problem? Do we understand the type of players that we need and the roles that they must fulfill? Have we assembled the right actors for these roles? Have we communicated what has to be done to achieve each objective? Have the options been practiced and rehearsed? Although these questions may appear to be common sense, common sense is one of the first things to vanish when the emergency is great and the stakes are high. As S. W. Erdnase states so eloquently at the beginning of this chapter: "Many experts with the gun who can nonchalantly ring up the bull's eye in a shooting gallery could not hit the side of a barn in a duel." Advantage Play executives are ones who can.

A D V A N T A G E   P L A Y

1. Advantage Play executives cannot afford to fantasize. They must deliver effective solutions in a casino environment each and every time.
2. Think not of what you can accomplish by yourself, but what you can accomplish as a team. Teamwork provides leverage and with leverage you can move the earth.
3. A team can only reap the rewards of Advantage Play if management knows how to assemble and direct its activities.
4. The Mechanics of Problem Solving provide a template for a simple game plan filled with detail and nuance.
5. Advantage Play executives assess and assemble team members carefully. They understand what motivates people to join a team and to perform to full potential.
6. Each member of the team must understand the mechanics of what he or she must do and how to *get into* and *get out of* what needs to be done.
7. Multiple options provide team members with the confidence needed to perform under pressure.
8. The team considers nothing too trivial that in any way contributes to its success.

9. Team members must practice individual techniques and rehearse the whole procedure in a real world environment before executing the plan.

10. Successful teams keep quiet so that they can continue to do business another day.

Forging the Future

Like acquiring many other feats, a perfect
understanding of the exact manner in
which it is performed will avoid the principal
difficulties. Practice will soon do the rest.

S. W. ERDNASE

I T WAS LATE NOVEMBER when I received the call. A friend had just received a summons to serve on a jury. The trial—a murder trial—was scheduled to take several weeks and the jury was to be sequestered. Even worse, the trial was scheduled for December—the prime cash flow season for entertainers. How, he asked, could he avoid jury duty? The solution flashed through my mind. "Tell the judge that you are not suitable to serve as a juror because you are psychic!" "So?" was his response. "So, because you are psychic, you *already* know the true state of mind of the accused!"

My friend attended the courtroom as scheduled and entered his request for dismissal. He asked to be excused from jury duty because although he was listed as an entertainer, he was actually a psychic entertainer and as such already knew whether or not the accused was guilty. The response of the court was predictable. The judge, lawyers, and accused all raised their heads. The judge, however, was very clever. He said,

"Do you get these impressions all of the time?" My friend responded, "No, but the impression is very strong right now." The judge concluded by saying, "Well, we have a different trial tomorrow. Come back and see how you feel about that one."

My friend returned the next day according to instructions. He was called into the judge's chambers—his office. The judge informed my friend that he had researched the matter. My friend need not prove that he had genuine psychic ability. There were grounds to exempt him from jury duty if his psychic beliefs made it impossible to render an impartial hearing of the evidence. Once again, the judge asked whether my friend held such beliefs. The response was affirmative and my friend then demonstrated the power of his ability by asking the judge to hold out his hand. The judge complied with the request and received a psychic reading about his past, present, and future. Astounded by the accuracy of the reading, the judge dismissed my friend from jury duty.

Now, how is that possible? Before I explain, let me offer my psychic impression of you.

I sense that you are a person of mature judgment. You are a person interested in other people and as such are perceptive and observant. You enjoy watching other people. You are not a physically aggressive person. Not only do you avoid physical violence—you would never harm another person intentionally—you are more likely to try to be of assistance to others.

A bit of a showperson, you enjoy being in the spotlight and have been on occasion the class clown or wit. Friends know, however, that you are open and direct about what you are doing when it is appropriate. You enjoy the company of others, probably because you have always had an attraction to others yourself and enjoyed a sense of personal power that comes from being popular. You are regarded as having a good sense of humor that is enjoyed by those around you. Despite your popularity, however, you pride yourself on fairness, particularly in your dealings with others.

People admire your dedication and diligence in developing your skills and abilities. The number two is important for you as you have a duality of being. Part of this duality is expressed in your work and public self. The other—which is quite different—is the private you. As a result, you are able to see things in people that others may miss. This is also one of the reasons why you are a very capable teacher when motivated. You have a high I.Q.—certainly above average—and this has enabled you to absorb a broad range of information on a variety of disciplines. Once again, however, there is a duality present. Your above-average intelligence enables you to grasp new and difficult concepts quickly but at times it is also the source of much frustration. You become frustrated when attempting to explain things to others who may not be as capable as yourself. Always remember that you are in the upper ranges of the population, and as such are more capable of seeing both the subjective and the objective sides of things.

This last point is very important, as it is the source of your balance as an individual. You see both the forest and the trees. The number two manifests itself in many other ways. You will have two loves in your life and two career opportunities. You tend to have two cars rather than one, and dare I say, two children. You will find this book to be of great value to you although you may not understand the power of the message until later on. It will add, however, to your ability to manage people and problems in a more creative way.

How did I do? Not too badly? Unfortunately, as you have probably surmised from the previous chapters, I do not possess the slightest psychic ability. I do, however, have many friends who are professional psychics. Unfortunately, none of them have any psychic ability either. Some are *mentalists*—people who use the technique of magicians to create the impression of psychic ability in the guise of entertainment; others are *readers*—people who use the same set of techniques as mentalists in order to provide psychic consulting services; and still others are *shut-eyes*—people who use the same set of techniques as those above but who have become so good at the process that they firmly believe they have genuine ability.

Although I have always been interested in the techniques used by professional psychics and spirit mediums, it took me a while to make the connection that they were, in fact, Advantage Players. The turning point came when I subscribed to a professional magazine called *Séance*. It sounded like an interesting read. Intrigued by the contents, I held my own séances to which I invited mediums and subjects—generally four or five hard-core believers, four or five skeptics, and a few in between. The format was always the same. A little red wine and cheese with some requiem music to establish the mood. Each person then sauntered off to have a personalized reading. Once everyone had had a reading, we would sit around the table to try to contact the dearly departed. The greatest revelation for me was the conversation after the individual readings were completed. Not only did people immediately compare notes—what did the psychic say about you—but most admitted, even those I thought initially were the most skeptical, that they sought their own psychic counsel on a regular basis. I had to learn more. I did.

A few years later I was invited to perform at a gathering to decide which country would host a major international exhibition. I was, in essence, the entertainment during a cocktail party where my client was lobbying intensely to be the successful bidder. I must admit there was some skepticism prior to the performance when I was introduced to other members of our team. Some of the politicians were more than a little nervous that a magician was part of the team. At a get-acquainted dinner before the major event, it was suggested that I perform a little magic to ease the concerns of the skeptics. Imagine my surprise after the performance when one of the most skeptical, a senior political figure and one of the most powerful backroom players in the country, quietly asked me whether or not I could tell fortunes. I said, "Of course!" He asked me to give him a reading then and there. I declined on the basis that we were in a very public place and readings are by their nature very intense and personal affairs. He then asked me if I would meet him in his hotel room around midnight. I accepted the invitation, attended as scheduled and told him about his past, his present, and, more importantly, his future. He had a problem he wanted solved. I solved it. It was then that I realized the power of the information I am about to disclose, information that represents post-graduate work in Advantage Play.

Psychics are consummate problem solvers. People turn to psychics for solutions. Think about it. Throughout history, humanity has tried to understand, predict, and control life and nature. People want not only certainty, but also an edge over others. As S. W. Erdnase suggests, "All men who play for any considerable stakes are looking for the best of it." They are more likely to seek this edge when they are under stress. Stress, of course, leads some people to gamble. It leads others who are uncertain or insecure to search for answers, contact, and support. Many people know the answer to their own problems. They just need to share their concerns with someone else. Psychics are basically hired listeners or rented friends. Authenticating the worth of the individual, of paying them attention, of helping them feel special is an important part of creative problem solving as it helps motivate people to solve problems, particularly their own.

Advantage Play executives and successful psychics share other characteristics. They are well organized, well read, and well briefed. They have a keen understanding of human emotion and what really troubles people. They have an eye for detail, are extremely observant, and are accomplished listeners. Most of all, they leave nothing to chance. They are incredibly proactive. They understand that their job is not so much to predict the future, but to make the future happen. This chapter outlines *the real work* on psychic readings. It presents a crash course in human nature, motivation, and the techniques Advantage Players use to shape it. Again, there are many details, each of which appears to be insignificant but when taken together create a powerful *effect*. Ultimately, Advantage Play executives can only be proficient at problem solving if they understand what motivates people and how to direct that motivation effectively.

So, how do psychics know the past, present, and future? The answer is simple. Although everyone likes to think of him- or herself as an individual, there is a *Pattern of Life* that all human beings follow. Each person suffers the same anxieties as others. The psychic determines where the client is in this Pattern of Life, which anxieties the client suffers from, and offers the client salvation or direction based on common sense. If the psychic is malevolent, the psychic offers prolonged sessions designed to cure or ward off evil.

Psychic analysis is powerful because it is purportedly based on some spiritual connection, not science. Most subjects believe that the psychic is able to do all of this because of some special gift rather than training and technique. Further, subjects assume that the psychic has no prior information about his or her affairs and that they do not provide the psychic with such information during the course of the reading.

The truth is somewhat different. Accurate readings are based on research, observation, and questioning all concealed under the guise of mysticism. It is only through such research, observation, and questioning that the psychic can provide guidance and make prognostications—prognostications based on a common sense understanding of cause and effect. Whether the psychic is using playing cards, tarot cards, stones, tea leaves, numerology, names, graphology (handwriting), astrology, or palmistry, each reading is structured the same. There is the pre-performance period of research and development that is concealed from the subject; the actual reading in which the psychic fine tunes his or her analysis of the subject and delivers the advice; and the final stage in which the psychic solidifies the value of the experience. Let's examine these three stages and see what lessons they provide for the Advantage Play executive.

Psychics know that the people who come to them have problems that they would like solved. This knowledge itself provides the psychic with a tremendous advantage. Once they know that they will be consulted because a message has been left or an appointment has been set, psychics prepare for their subject. The psychic obtains as much information as possible about the client *before* the client shows up for the consultation by consulting the Creative Infrastructure.

Many years ago the psychic Creative Infrastructure was a blue book that circulated among professional psychics containing personal information about clients and their beliefs. Just as an organization's base level of knowledge increases with the exchange of information, so too the accuracy of a psychic reading increased with the exchange of the blue book. The blue book of information exists today electronically and can now circumnavigate the globe in an instant via the Internet. The Internet also furnishes the psychic with unparalleled information about companies, people, genealogical studies, and credit history.

You may recall "advantages that are bound to ultimately

give a percentage in favor of the professional are absolutely essential to his existence." The psychic hunts for any piece of information that provides an edge. One professional psychic requires that new clients provide him with a credit card number in order to secure a time slot for a personal reading. This credit card number provides a key to surreptitiously unlocking personal secrets, secrets that may be regurgitated back to the client during a reading to impress the client with the power of the reader. Other forms of payment can provide just as much advance information. A check, for example, can reveal a great deal of personal information about the subject, all of which the professional psychic will add to the client file that forms part of the Creative Infrastructure.

Many checks show a three- or four-digit number printed to the right of the name and address of the payee. This number indicates when the person opened the account. Thus, the number 1-99 indicates that a person opened the account in January of 1999. This number may also indicate the date of some major change in the life of the subject. Why, after all, do most people open new bank accounts? Have they moved? Are they separated? Has there been a divorce?

The subject's address as printed on the check can also be a source of much information. Not only does it provide the psychic with information about the neighborhood in which the subject resides, it may provide other useful information when placed in context. For example, if it bears an address that is different than the address that is printed on the envelope in which it was delivered, it may point to a similar change in lifestyle— a move, a separation, a divorce.

And what about the name on the check? Is there one name or two? One name often indicates single status. Two names indicate some sort of relationship. Are the last names the same? Married, common law, or token independence?

A check may bear a hallmark of a credit union, hospital, or benevolent society. What does that tell you? Its overall design may range from plain—a frugal person trying to save a few pennies by refusing to order customized checks—to pre-printed wildlife, floral, or industrial tableaus that imply some cultural sophistication on the payer but in reality provide a thumbnail portrait of the personality of the account holder. Finally, size does matter. Personal checks, for example, are usually smaller than business checks. Also, a postdated check may be a sign that the payer might be experiencing some financial stress even if it is something as simple as waiting for a deposit to clear.

The pièce de résistance is the phone number. Think of how easy it is once the psychic has a phone number to seek personal information based on the premise of a marketing survey. So much information—each morsel of which provides the professional psychic with an added advantage—from a simple everyday article of commerce.

Psychics also resort to less nefarious research methods. It is not uncommon to ask the client to complete a simple survey or questionnaire upon entering the studio. The client, however, is asked to give the survey to the psychic after the session. Unbeknownst to the client, however, the clipboard that holds the questionnaire—and that the client assumes is there to provide a surface for completing the document—contains a sheet of carbon paper beneath its veneer. The psychic or assistant retrieves the clipboard from the client, secretly removes the carbon, and reviews the information prior to the main reading. The questionnaire can provide the psychic with all the information needed to ensure an accurate reading—name, address, phone number, social insurance number, astrological sign, and even the reason for the visit.

One of the most powerful pieces of information in the hands of the psychic is the U.S. Social Security number because the first three digits indicate where the person first applied for and received the number. The psychic will quickly ascertain this information to see whether the client has moved from that particular jurisdiction. Clients are impressed when told that not only have they moved, but also the state from which they relocated.

My friend was able to secure his release from jury duty because he convinced the judge of his psychic ability. His psychic analysis, however, was based firmly on empirical research. Knowing that he would have to return to the courthouse the next day, my friend visited the courthouse law library, looked up the profile of the judge in the who's who of the legal directories, and learned a great deal about the judge's past and present activities, including where he was born, to whom he was married, major papers he had written, the firm where he had practiced law prior to becoming a judge, and the date he was called to the bench. He recycled this information in a subtle manner as he purportedly mapped out the judge's life based on the lifeline in the palm of the judge's hand.

In a world where there are six degrees of separation

between you and anyone else, it is quite easy to obtain inside information. When I entered the hotel room at midnight to give a private personal reading to the political figure, I had two distinct advantages. I grew up in a political family and have followed political events closely. I knew all about this man, his past, and his present. Second, even though my home was hundreds of miles away from his, I knew what was going on in his household. I was privy to this information through sheer happenstance. My subject had just had a change of domestic situation and was living in the home of another major political figure—whose niece happened to be a neighbor. So, without even knowing that we would meet on this junket, or that he had any interest in the psychic world, or that he would ask me to give him a private reading, I was ready. Ultimately I gave him the advice that any true friend would have given him in the circumstances. I told him to retire from politics, not because he was of a different political stripe from me— which he was—but because he was tired and burnt out and had other challenges in life. I told him that his successor—whom he himself had groomed—was in place and was ready to take charge. All of which was true. Finally, I told him about his new love interest and the need, at this juncture in his life, to devote more time to developing this relationship than being the master of political intrigue. He obviously agreed.

Even though the psychic may have done tremendous research on his client, he still seeks additional advantages prior to conducting the initial reading. Creating the appropriate environment is one such advantage. A psychic without the accoutrements of mysticism is like a law firm without the marble foyer. The advice may be the same but the perception of its value is quite different. Old books, candles, new age music, tarot cards, and crystal balls all contribute to placing the client in the right state of mind. Clients are more likely to believe in the prognostications if they are delivered in a manner that is consistent with their perception of the process. Second, tarot cards and crystal balls not only add to the atmosphere but also provide a focal point for misdirection or *shade* that creates an alternative reality. The client who stares at the cards or the ball will not notice that the psychic is, in fact, observing for telltale signs indicating the accuracy of his statements.

The size of the fee is another factor that provides an additional advantage. A large fee discourages the merely curious and attracts those who already believe in psychics and psychic phenomena. Even with all of this in place, the professional psychic still has one other extremely important task to perform before commencing the initial reading: observation and analysis of the client.

There is no better source of information about the client and his or her problem than the client him- or herself. It is all there to observe. As Advantage Players, psychics are observant, constantly looking for *tells* that provide them with additional information that can be used to their advantage. Observing a client from the top down means starting with the head. Is the hair natural in color compared to the eyebrows? Is it stylish or is it cut conservatively? Does the client wear glasses or earrings or sport other piercing? Is there much make-up? Do the eyes show fatigue and are the lips chapped? The psychic then observes the clothing. If clothes make the man, what does the style, color, and fabric tell us about the individual. How do they fit? Has the client lost or put on weight? Are the pockets loaded with objects? Does the client look meticulous or careless? Now, how about the hands? Are they smooth and well-manicured or are they rough and callused? Is he or she wearing a signet, class, or fraternity ring? What about a wedding band? Is it on or does it look as though it was removed recently? If on, would the ring be difficult to remove? Is the introductory handshake firm and authoritative or tentative and meek? What about the shoes? Do they work with the outfit? How about the color, style, cost, and care? Do they look maintained? Are the shoes indicative of a particular job or occupation?

Observation continues. Does the client display any badges of identification? Is there a crucifix, a Star of David, an astrological sign, or a name dangling from a chain? What about a BMW key chain? What did the client bring to the session? A magazine? Papers from work? A notebook computer? The observation and analysis of these *tells* provide a great deal of non-verbal personal information. The trained observer will absorb all of this information. It is a psychic roadmap for the reading. Best of all, it has taken place before anyone is aware that the presentation has started. Clients delude themselves into thinking that psychics are able to divine information at first instance through some extra-sensory gift. Once the psychic has conducted this research and made preliminary observations about the client, it is time to start the reading.

The reading may begin with a simple psychic experiment designed to establish a rapport with the client.

Once a rapport has been established, the psychic will offer a focal point for misdirection. Would the client prefer a reading based on the tarot, astrology, numerology, tea leaves, rune stones, palmistry, or psychometrics? It is immaterial to the psychic and to the prognostications. Regardless of which system of divination is employed, the psychic will deliver a *Universal Read*—a profile of the client's past, present, and future delivered in general terms but interpreted by the client as pertinent or appropriate to just them. Advantage Play executives realize that to motivate a person, they must demonstrate that they understand the past.

This Universal Read is quite sophisticated. It contains many ambiguous statements that are clarified unconsciously by the client. These ambiguous statements touch upon areas that concern most people— travel, health, expectations, sex, career, ambition, and money—T.H.E. S.C.A.M.—as they move through the Pattern of Life.

As the psychic delivers The Universal Read, he observes the reaction to each ambiguous statement, as the reactions tip what troubles and motivates the individual. The psychic can then use this information along with the knowledge obtained through prior research and observation to craft a compelling presentation. The psychic is an Advantage Player who has created a Multiple Option Universe. The psychic is prepared to alter the form and flow of this presentation based on the conditions that arise during the meeting and is truly responsive to situational conditions.

Let me illustrate this process by outlining both a Universal Read and the Pattern of Life. I will then inventory the *tells* a client may provide that, in turn, direct the Advantage Player in the advice he or she provides.

THE UNIVERSAL READ

"I am glad that you have taken this opportunity to consult with me, because I definitely feel that I can touch upon the conditions that trouble you, and help you overcome them. I must know in advance, however, whether you want me to include the very dark. Everyone has a unique disposition. I must know. Very well.

"I feel at the present, you are troubled—troubled in your mind. There is confusion. You know that you must soon make a decision but are not sure exactly which way to turn. You know that the situation calls for clear thinking and logical decisions but the fact that there are two paths—two options—makes it difficult. Right now both paths are lonely because you have not really confided in anyone else the depth of the problem. You are alone with just your thoughts. To determine which path is the right path, we must look at the large picture.

"Decision making is impeded by your domestic and financial affairs. Neither are progressing as well as you hoped they would be. Something is holding you back. You are coming up just a little short of your goal. For all the effort and energy you have invested, the results should be better. You will only make proper progress, however, if you can throw off this yoke and express your true self.

"Although you feel isolated, you know there are others around you—many people—most of whom are true friends. In fact, one person stands out in particular. This person has a great deal of influence over you and others. This person is both the source of your worry and anxiety and—I see—the best source of salvation. You must put the worry on the shelf in order to reach the root of the trouble. Only once you have done this will you be able to analyze it and follow the right path. This disturbing element—which has caused you much frustration, delay, and uncertainty—can be removed easily.

"On a positive note, you have much personal magnetism and this can be a big factor in over-coming obstacles. Beware, however, the power to charm and fascinate others. It is within you but you are also susceptible to the charm and influence of others—much to your own detriment. You are in a cycle of unsettled conditions, which is slowly but surely changing for the better. Don't wait to see what happens. Reason tells you what is required. You can be master of your own destiny.

"You have time to achieve all that you want. I perceive an energy around you that indicates a long life. You will most likely live longer than most members of your family—possibly to the age of eighty to eighty-five years. You will experience your share of ups and downs but they will be minor. Your life should be reasonably free of personal injuries, serious illness, and accidents. Take care to avoid a nervous condition and a stomach

disorder. By proper living and care, these things will take care of themselves and you will also avoid a glandular disturbance late in life.

"I sense your concern about financial conditions. They have never proven to be entirely satisfactory. Retirement is an issue. I see that you want to improve this situation. You believe, however, that you have been restrained. These restraints make your goals outside of your reach. Remember that your life will experience many cycles and that this current one has almost passed. Financial conditions will improve in the near future. I sense more money—through better conditions. This improved condition will come partly through a friend—a true friend who will help you. They will help you by recognizing how much they depend on you. They will depend on you even more but it will be to your mutual advantage.

"Your quest for stability will lead you to make an investment in real estate. This will prove to be quite beneficial down the line. The key is to overcome the feeling of uncertainty and frustration. Only then will you be able to manage your own affairs. Much progress will be made. Again, this change will come and be of much help.

"On a personal note, have you suffered a near tragedy or great loss? I thought so. These moments of tears and sorrow have been accompanied by frustrations—frustration that things might have been different if you had had more control. You will gain more control as you grow older because your experience brings balance in your life and

you will be able to forge your own path toward greater happiness.

"The opposite sex is friendlier to you than your own sex. Not as threatened. In fact, I see one—maybe two—persons have had an especially strong influence on you. You care about this person very much. Correct? As I go deeper, your heart is heavy because you feel you have been denied. Not many perceive this. You have sort of a double life—one is physical and the other is in your imagination. You must use judgment, however, and make logical decisions that will bring about your secret desires and ambitions to life.

"There is something—something that keeps the two of you apart. You can't put your finger on it. It doesn't matter how hard you try, your efforts are not noticed. Or if they are noticed, they are not appreciated. Is this not correct? This person is influenced by others. This unfavorable influence can be removed.

"I said earlier that there might be a second person. Medium height—dark hair. Not sure whether or not you can trust this person as a true friend. Your own intuition tells you that you could be deceived by this person. Correct? Wait. There is another. More fair—and this person can provide friendship and influence over others. Look for this person. Open up or cultivate this relationship as it will mean much to you in the future. Beware, however, of jealous people. They will be jealous of you, your friends, and your success. This must be of concern later on. They are not

*currently in a position to do you any harm. Just
be careful.*

*"As one cycle follows another, you will be able
to make decisions quickly and firmly. There will
be less confusion in your mind. Part of this will be
due to your experience, but part—more than most
would imagine—will be from your own intuitive
or psychic nature. You know that your own
impressions and premonitions have nearly always
been correct, and yet you have not followed them.
This will change in the future. You will also be
able to help other people with this gift. For now,
however, be mindful of these impressions as they
generally always put you on the right path. You
will be able to see deception and avoid much
unhappiness if you place more value on your own
inherent gifts.*

*"Married—more than once. First one okay but
lacking in many of the things that you know are
possible. The second—much more fulfilling. Money
also comes into it. You will receive some—not a lot
(there is no early retirement) but enough to make a
difference, be appreciated, and put to good use.
You will experience some delays, however, accessing this money. Possible legal dispute. You win and
your victory is more than worth the effort. Just be
careful signing any piece of paper that you do not
completely understand. This may not make much
sense now but remember it. You will recognize the
importance of it later on.*

*"You will receive word—from someone else—
verbally—that will surprise you. Although neither*

bad nor good, it could have a significant impact on your life. Sometimes inactivity is just as powerful as activity. You know that someone is watching over you.

"In matters of the heart—there are several tremors. Love, not disease. Love does surround you and the sooner you recognize it, the more it will make up for all the love you thought you missed earlier in life. It can be yours. It belongs to you. Don't be disappointed or melancholy if things do not go right. Not only does this hamper your progress but it puts additional strain on your health. Even though you sometimes let emotions run from the high to the low—sometimes to the depths of despair—you should not let disappointment consume you. Disappointment will pass as the cycle continues. Accelerate the transition by drawing on the reserve of positive energy that you know resides within you. Although this year has been a good year, the next three will be even better—offering you more than you have enjoyed in the past if you let it. As your best day of the week is Monday, major undertakings, transactions, and changes should be scheduled early in the week.

"Eventually you will acquire much wealth. You will not be in need or distress. For now, avoid antagonism—it makes you blue. Turn the energy around, follow the path you know is right and there will be balance, harmony, and success.

"Now, I have not touched upon some other matters, so if you have specific questions, focus on the most important one and we can discuss it."

This reading will be augmented throughout by the information provided to the psychic by the client. The concept of the Universal Read has evolved over the years. Obviously, the more research the psychic has conducted prior to the initial reading, the more it can be tailored towards his target. The reading offered at the beginning of this chapter was based on the profile of the type of person who is interested in problem solving, creativity, and sales, and buys books on these subjects. The Universal Read just provided is for a more generic audience.

To be an effective psychic, the reader must manage people, procedures, and information. Hundreds of minute and apparently inconsequential details are added together to create a powerful and potentially life-changing experience. Again, psychics do not predict the future; they make it happen. Let's look at some of the tasks in more detail.

First, the psychic must place the client in the Pattern of Life. What is the Pattern of Life? Life starts with childbirth. Everyone was an infant at one time. Most infants suffer a set range of diseases and ailments. Chances of survival are great after the child has passed its first year of life. From age six to seventeen, the focus for most children is on education. Education broadens significantly with puberty as children come to terms with their own sexuality. Most people remember a childhood romance. It lingers in the memory. Children begin to reason for themselves, demonstrating their ability to cope with reality one way or another as they seek greater independence. The child may demonstrate adequacy in positive or negative terms. The child matures physically, achieves more education, and adopts a more active lifestyle—participating in more extracurricular activities, sports, and pastimes and in a larger social network.

The psychic is like an actuary. He or she will be familiar with statistics on everything from the percentage of people who obtain a high school education to the percentage of people who attend and then complete post-secondary study. The psychic knows that most children who fail to attend a post-secondary institution are likely to take some occupational endeavor or work in some menial or low-service activity. Romance, of course, leads to relationships. Psychics know the age at which most women marry, the success rate for most marriages, and how that rate is altered by the presence of children. Statistics are the life-blood of the profession.

Children play an important role in the Pattern of Life. To have or have not?—that is the question. Marriages with children usually last longer because of the pressure of maintaining a home. Relationships are stressful. Children only add to the pressure. People must find accommodation—perhaps buy a house—and acquire material goods. They have entered the consumption phase in the Pattern of Life. Efforts are doubled: must be aggressive, work harder, obtain a promotion, spend, and save. Economic and emotional pressures mount. Stress increases. Few people accept their lot in life. They hope for something better and live with the thought of lost opportunities. The latter stages of life are full of worry: health, security, retirement, and loneliness. Can they finance the lifestyle to which they have become accustomed or to which they aspire? Distance and death and responsibility to others only add to the tension. People become aware of their own mortality.

This is just the pattern that most people follow. It is helpful to know this pattern even if you have no intention of conducting psychic readings. It gives you an appreciation of what you, your family, friends, and colleagues may be going through at a particular time. Advantage Play executives take comfort in the knowledge that even though the problems each person encounters seem unique, they are shared by most as they move through life. Businesses also have their own Pattern of Life. They start up, have growing pains, sometimes marry, have children, reach maturity, and fade into the distance.

Psychics couple their knowledge of the Pattern of Life with research and observation to get *one-ahead* of their clients. This is an important principle of Advantage Play. Coined originally by magicians, it means that while the spectator is waiting for effect number one, the magician has already set the stage for that *effect* and is secretly setting the stage for *effect* number two. By working *one-ahead*—sometimes *two-ahead*—the magician has neatly separated the link between *cause* and *effect,* making it almost impossible for the audience to reconstruct the modus operandi for each individual effect. The psychic is doing the same thing, preparing for the second stage while performing the first. The client assumes that the psychic is divining information in real time—that is, while the cards are being turned over or the lines in the palm are being traced. The psychic, however, is ahead in the game. As the psychic is saying his or her piece, he or she is multi-tasking—being an active listener and an astute observer of human behavior in order to alter the future course of his or her presentation to the needs of the client. It is *The Trick That Cannot Be Explained* revisited.

To personalize the reading, the psychic must determine what particular problems plague the client. Once again, the problems may be remembered by the anagram T – H – E – S – C – A – M. Most people are concerned with **T**ravel, **H**ealth, **E**xpectations, **S**ex, **C**areer, **A**mbition, and **M**oney. Most psychics—if pressed—reduce human anxiety down to one source— sex! People are anxious because they either have too much—multiple partners and secret affairs—or not enough (with wife, partner, or object of desire in the workplace), all of which create additional stress on time, energy, finances, and other resources. The psychic must determine where the client is in the Pattern of Life, secretly determine which issues are of most concern, and then dispense advice appropriate to the client and the ethics of the psychic.

So how does the psychic determine which issues are of most concern to his or her client? The answer is threefold. First, the psychic is an active listener. Unconsciously the client describes what it is that is bothering him or her in response to some stimulus provided by the psychic during the reading. Psychics depend on clients interjecting comments. It is one of the main reasons that the client visits the psychic in the first place. He or she wants to confide in anyone who will listen. Active listening includes analyzing the tone of the voice and the delivery of the words. Do not underestimate the power and effectiveness of listening.

The psychic will also look for *tells*, those physiological signs that indicate the psychic has hit an area of concern to the subject during the reading. The client may fidget, cross his or her legs, lean forward or backward, dip the forehead, or all of the above. One well-respected psychic advocates conducting the reading on a glass-top table in order to observe the body language beneath the table, the subject shifting in the chair, or crossing or uncrossing legs, which are physiological signs that indicate a hit. This same psychic advocates putting clients in squeaky swivel chairs—ones that may produce a slight squeak with every movement—in order to highlight each hit. Tarot cards or crystal balls also provide a distinct advantage. By directing the focus of attention on these articles, the psychic is free to observe the body language of the client, gauging the reaction to each component of the read. Palm reading provides the same advantage. The psychic holds the hand of the client and physically monitors the reaction to the presentation. Remember that Advantage Players use every artifice that can tip the odds in their favor.

Third, the psychic asks questions—direct questions that could be interpreted in several ways—but always concealed in the guise of a statement. The statement "You have a partner," for example, can be interpreted as an assertion or as a question. Further, the word "partner" can be interpreted in a variety of ways: spouse, business colleague, lover. What the client may interpret as a question that requires an answer can always be described in hindsight as an assertion. You have a partner! The psychic observes the impression the question makes on the subject and then creates the impression that he or she only had one option or path in mind when uttering the phrase. Advantage Play executives use the same techniques to determine what concerns and motivates people.

Once the psychic knows the problem, he or she must give advice, but what advice? Making predictions can be a dangerous game, particularly for people who really believe in psychic phenomena. Stewart James learned this lesson in a dramatic fashion. The year was 1938. Stewart was a feature performer at a gathering of magicians near Niagara Falls, Ontario. The convention was not far geographically from Lilly Dale, New York— an epicenter for psychics and spiritualists. In order to obtain publicity for his gathering of magicians, Bob Weill, the producer of the event, challenged the spiritualist camp. Stewart James would perform something that the spiritualists could not duplicate. Stewart would predict the headline of the local newspaper one year in advance of publication—the date coinciding with the next year's gathering of magicians in the area. Originally Weill was going to propose that Stewart James would duplicate with natural means any psychic or spiritualistic manifestation presented by the spiritualists but was persuaded by Stewart to alter the challenge. What if, Stewart pondered, the spiritualists could do something that he could not duplicate—not because it was psychic but because he could not figure out their trickery? Stewart was confident, however, none in the spiritualist camp could duplicate the headline prediction. He himself had no idea of how to perform it. At least he had a year to figure it out. So, Stewart scrawled his prediction on a piece of paper, rolled it up, and inserted the roll in a block of wood that was subsequently locked and put

into the possession of the local authorities. He vowed he
would return at the next year's gathering of magicians
where the prediction would be revealed.

Stewart did return the following year and presented
himself to the police so that he could be incarcerated
prior to the publication date of the newspaper. Stewart
could not get to or tamper with the message deposited
in the block of wood. Just prior to show time, the police
escorted Stewart from the cell to the stage. The block of
wood was opened, the chief of police unrolled the
paper, and read it out loud: Germany invades Poland.
Stewart's prediction was correct. He predicted the out-
break of World War II. The *effect* was so startling and the
headline of such importance that Stewart obtained
national coverage.

Despite his protestations to the contrary, people
believed Stewart was a genuine psychic. People
pestered Stewart for other prognostications. The only
thing Stewart knew for certain was that he had no psychic ability whatsoever. He was spooked—no pun
intended—by the cries for help and willingness of people to check rationality at the door. Alarmed by the
attention the prediction created, he promised to himself
that he would never grandstand a psychic belief again.

Professional psychics, however, are required to
make predictions. Clients expect predictions. More
importantly, the predictions must have some accuracy or
the client will not return for more. Psychics face commercial constraints like any other business. Like other
professionals, 80 percent of their income is derived from
20 percent of their client base. Some psychics are more
flamboyant than others, sensationalizing the perform-

ance to create a reputation, a natural by-product of our competitive age—think advertising, think lawyers, think contractors—most predictions are made to inspire confidence and attract customers. Psychic predictions are based on a third-party objective appraisal of cause and effect. Once the psychic discovers the cause of the problem, it is easy to predict the remedy. The psychic builds the practice by providing common sense suggestions that most people have failed to call upon. Psychics are professional problem solvers. The psychic has the advantage. He or she has studied the client's life and, like any therapist, is usually in a better position to predict the probable course of events. Clients are impressed by the vision because they themselves do not know their own minds, otherwise they would not be seeking psychic counsel in the first place. Psychics keep predictions within the realm of probability. Not only are reasonable predictions more likely to be accepted by the client, they might even inspire—giving the client new hope and promise—to achieve the goal now within reach. There are, of course, exceptions. Less scrupulous psychics frighten their clients. They perceive evil, misfortune, and bad luck all around. Remedies are available but only at a price—multiple sessions and various talismans. Advantage Play executives make predictions based on research, reality, and a common sense appraisal of *cause* and *effect.*

Now that you understand how the psychic reading unfolds, we can examine the reasons why such readings are so effective and discover the application these principles have in a broader context. We want to separate the principles of deception from the act of deception in order to increase our own inventory of expertise.

The techniques used by psychics are successful for a variety of reasons. First, even though the Universal Read is stocked with generalities, most people accept such general personality descriptions as being accurate for themselves. Psychologists have dubbed this the "P.T. Barnum Effect." People tend to focus their perceptions upon those aspects of information that fit with their existing mindset. Most people interpret information—particularly ambiguous information—in a manner consistent with their current beliefs. People accept any statement that is reasonable and positive, particularly if the message is delivered with confidence. Psychics have dominant personalities and most subjects will try to comply with the demand characteristics of the situation and try to be good subjects. Psychics can deliver prognostications with power because the client cannot disagree. The client cannot contradict, regardless of how fantastic the reading or prediction of the future event may be, for the simple reason that neither one can really know what will happen.

Psychics depend on their clients having selective recall. They will recall the hits more than the misses, and they will forget that the readings were full of words for which the client—not the psychic—defined the meaning. People are more inclined to acquiesce when they are uncertain of their perceptions. Perception is an act of synthesis, and when the stimulus is ambiguous, the perceiver rather than the transmitter determines the meaning.

Psychic readings also work when the psychic makes statements like "You do not like to be ordered around.

You will cooperate willingly if asked but dislike being bossed around." These statements apply to just about everyone, as most people react strongly against imperative commands. Such commands psychologically threaten personal freedom. Self-fulfilling prophecies are also of assistance psychologically in that, when a person has expectations, he or she will look for data that confirms that expectation. Thus, telling someone that she is going to come by some money or meet a tall, dark, and handsome person may create a search for such an event. Finally, psychics with a reputation carry more weight simply because people with a reputation can compel consent, approval, or acquiescence regardless of the merits of their argument.

As discussed in conjunction with Advantage Sales, reputations often are created because people misremember detail. Psychics capitalize on the phenomenon of *false memory* to enhance their work. The professional psychic, for example, does everything within his or her power for the client to remember the hits rather than the misses. The psychic wants the client to provide continual unsolicited testimonials about his or her abilities.

I have tried to provide information not only on how psychics structure the readings and operate their businesses, but also why people are so quick to praise their successes. Some may be offended that I have deconstructed the process in such clinical detail. They may say, "That may be true of fraudulent psychics, but my psychic is genuine." As Joseph Dunninger, America's foremost psychic entertainer, was fond of saying, "To those who believe, no explanation is necessary. To those who do not believe, no explanation is possible."

Although I would love to meet someone with real powers of prognostication, I remain skeptical. I believe that each individual is the architect of his or her own destiny.

Advantage Players are effective because they research not only the client's individual history but also the life cycle of the market in which they operate. Only by being informed can they place a problem in the appropriate context and offer tangible solutions based on an educated understanding of cause and effect. Advantage Players are effective because they listen—actively—and look for *tells* that reveal the innermost thoughts and feelings of their personnel and their customers. Advantage Players know that a well-crafted suggestion carries more weight than a command. Advantage Players are cognizant of the environment in which they work and set the stage appropriately so that the setting supports the strength of their remarks.

Although people or colleagues may credit the Advantage Play executive with psychic intuition in delivering solutions, the real secret may be as simple as being well prepared, observant, and an active listener; and tabling solutions based on common sense and understanding the cycle of the project or enterprise. Putting it into practice means providing leadership. Instead of looking at a crystal ball, dealing cards, reading horoscopes and tea leaves, Advantage Players make predictions based on the probability of incremental change, and that can be orchestrated by an individual who receives positive encouragement so that events become self-fulfilling prophecies. Advantage Players make it happen.

A D V A N T A G E   P L A Y

1. Do not predict the future, make it happen.
2. Make sure your working environment is consistent with your mandate.
3. To understand business, you must understand people, the *Pattern of Life*, and what motivates them.
4. People are motivated by THE SCAM: Travel, Health, Expectations, Sex, Career, Ambition, and Money.
5. Research, observe, analyze, and predict incremental change based on cause and effect.
6. No piece of information, contact, or casual remark is trivial.
7. Look for *tells*—signs that indicate you are on the right course of action.
8. Beware of ambiguous stimulus—as they force people to make their own self-fulfilling prophecies rather than fulfilling your predictions.
9. It is better to lead information so that people come to the conclusions you want rather than imposing your will from above.
10. Look for stress and strain in people and communicate with them internally rather than force them to seek outside counsel from psychics.

Perfect Practice

*Many hours of incessant practice must be
spent to acquire the requisite amount of skill;
but it must be remembered if feats at card-
handling could be attained for the asking
there would be little in such performance to
interest or profit any one.*

S. W. ERDNASE

A S A YOUNG MAN GROWING UP in Ottawa, Canada,
Dai Vernon dreamed of New York City. He had
a taste of the city in 1913, when he was nineteen years
old. He was determined to move there and did so in
1915, after convincing his family that he was going to
study art at the Art Students' League. His heart, however,
was into magic. The economic climate for entertainers
was not favorable. Vernon's name (then Verner) soon
made a trade paper, albeit with some degree of derision
on the part of the publisher.

Broadway Chatter
By ONE OF THE BOYS

*Fred Griffith—"I've cut out all magic except the billiard
balls."*

Al Anderson—"Magic isn't my vocation, it's my vacation."

Poole—"Oh, yes, I work now and then." Ad lib, "Mostly then."

Ziska—"One more whack and then I'm through."

Green—"It's all a matter of luck."

Verner (fresh from Canada)—"You're all a bunch of pessimists. The chap with the goods will make good."

Vernon was the chap with the goods and as such would transform the world of magic. Although Vernon's life was filled with colorful characters and packed with amazing stories, one story in particular—his search for an elusive card sleight—epitomizes the drive, skill, and philosophy of the Advantage Player, and it is a fitting way to conclude our study of Advantage Play.

In January 1932, Vernon was in Wichita, Kansas, plying his other trade—cutting silhouettes—for the Innes Department Store. Vernon was regarded as a virtuoso with shears. The *New York Times* proclaiming, "His silhouettes will mark an era," and The *New York Telegraph* commenting, "There will come a time when a Vernon silhouette will be a treasure. He is the best exponent of the art we have ever come across." In fact, soon Vernon would be engaged by the famous Billy Rose to perform magic and cut silhouettes at his exclusive New York night club, the Casino de Paris. For now, however, he was in Wichita, Kansas. Cutting silhouettes gave him the opportunity to visit friends and make some money during the Depression.

Wichita, Kansas, was the closest major center to St. Joseph, Missouri—the home of a dedicated amateur

magician named Faucett Ross. Ross would later become
the Boswell to Vernon's Johnson. They had first met in
New York in 1927, and Vernon thought that January
1932 was a good time to get reacquainted. Vernon
arrived in Wichita with his wife Jeanne and their young
son Edward.

Although Vernon was supposed to be cutting silhouettes, he spent most of his time practicing and discussing
magic with Faucett Ross. The crowd at the department
store would just have to wait a little longer for the artistic renderings cut from black paper. One afternoon when
Vernon actually was at work, Faucett Ross rushed in with
some startling news. A Mexican was involved in a shooting and was being held in the local jail. More important,
the Mexican was a gambler who was passing the time in
the cell demonstrating his dexterity with the pasteboards.
Vernon was ready to hold the crowd in the department
store in abeyance. Ross, however, said the Mexican was-
n't going anywhere and that he had arranged for the two
of them to meet him later that evening.

Vernon had been intrigued by Advantage Players
since childhood. From his initial discovery of *Erdnase* at
the age of eight to the teenager finding doctored decks of
cards scattered along the railroad tracks near Ottawa—
evidence of an illicit card game gone awry—he dreamed
of what it would be like to be an Advantage Player. He
could only imagine the adventure. As he matured, he met
some of these players. On occasion he would meet a virtuoso like Dad Stevens—an old Mississippi gambler
whom Vernon met in Chicago in 1919, and whose manip-
ulative skill with the pasteboards literally brought tears to
Vernon's eyes. While other times he would meet penny-

ante players whose only skill was a particular sleight or move that always *got the money*. Vernon was interested in them all. He admired their technical prowess, capacity for management, and their ability to perform under pressure. Vernon would travel far and wide and on little information to find arcane knowledge that he could add to his Creative Infrastructure. As Advantage Players are reluctant to release their secrets, Vernon would use his own considerable skills with cards to pry each elusive secret from its holder.

Vernon and Ross met the Mexican incarcerated in the local jail. The gambler performed little that Vernon had not seen before. Vernon then asked the gambler if he had seen anything unusual in his travels. Upon reflection, the gambler told Vernon that he had once seen a man who could deal cards secretly from the center of the deck.

How could this be? Only once in his career had Vernon heard of the concept of dealing from the center of the deck. It was in the 1920s when another card man—John Sprong from Chicago—notified Vernon that he had heard a rumor that someone in the Midwest could deal from the center. Vernon dismissed it as a fairy tale. Sprong, however, offered money to anyone who could point him toward the person who possibly could do such a thing. Nothing, however, became of it. No one—not even Vernon—could do such a sleight. But here in Wichita, Vernon was speaking with someone who had actually witnessed it. Perhaps it was possible.

If it was possible to perform the center deal, the sleight would be the Holy Grail for the Advantage Player. Current practice required card players to give the player on the right the opportunity to cut the cards prior to the deal. This posed a significant hurdle for those who prefer to deal the second or bottom card of the pack as it buries the known cards in the center of the deck. To short-circuit the cut, the Advantage Player must either employ a secret ally to cut the cards at the desired location or he must *shift* the deck, that is secretly transpose the halves after the cut to restore them to their original position. Both strategies have their shortcomings. The ally costs money and may talk and the shift is almost impossible to perform in fast company. S. W. Erdnase himself wrote, "The shift has yet to be invented that can be executed by a movement appearing as coincident card-table routine." Dealing from the center of the deck by secretly drawing out the required cards from where they lie in pack after an arm's-length party has cut the cards was clearly the solution. If it could be performed in a manner that, as Erdnase would say, "the most critical observer would not even suspect, let alone detect," then you would be guaranteed to *get the money*.

Vernon interrogated the Mexican. Where did he see it? How did it look? Were there any *tells*? What did the player look like? Did he know his name? The Mexican offered little information. Yes, the deal looked perfect. There were no *tells*. He saw it performed in Kansas City by a man who appeared to be slightly younger than Vernon. The Mexican could provide no other information. For Vernon, the course was clear: drop everything, head off to Kansas City, and find this man who could deal from the center of the deck.

Vernon had a formidable challenge. It is one thing to track down an Advantage Player; it is another to get him to divulge his innermost secrets. Kansas City, in particular, was teeming with gambling dens and out-of-town hustlers. It was also the home of the K.C. Card Co., one of the leading suppliers of gambling equipment, both legal and illegal, to the profession. Illicit gambling was *the* industry in Kansas City and as such was protected by organized crime. Finding the man would be like finding the needle in the proverbial haystack. Just before Vernon embarked on this journey, Charles E. Miller arrived on his doorstep. Twenty-two years of age, Miller had come from El Paso, Texas, to visit Faucett Ross. His real purpose, however, was to meet the legend named Dai Vernon. Vernon was so impressed with the skill of the youth that Miller joined the hunt. It would be Vernon, however, who did all the talking.

They searched every bar, poolroom, and backroom joint. At each junction and with every new contact, Vernon and Miller had to prove they were neither government agents nor rivals from another mob. This proved particularly difficult at times because Vernon was so steeped in knowledge of card players and card table artifice that many concluded only a government agent could be privy to such an extraordinary amount of information. When an entrée was made and Vernon asked the question, "Do you know anyone who can deal from the center of the deck?" people shook their heads in startled disbelief and said, "You must be crazy. No one can deal from the center of the deck." Vernon and Miller began to think that perhaps it was just an urban myth. Miller abandoned the search and headed back to El Paso, Texas. Vernon returned to his family in Wichita but vowed he would continue the search.

He did return shortly afterwards to Kansas City and renewed his quest, starting once again at the K.C. Card Co. Hanging around the shop, Vernon demonstrated his own particular prowess with the pasteboards and even showcased a few of the gambling accoutrements he himself had picked up in his travels across America. The employees impressed. Once again he pressed them for information about the center deal. The employees of the K.C. Card Co. could only suggest that Vernon contact an old-time gambler of their acquaintance. If anyone would know, he might be the man. Vernon eagerly followed the new lead.

Vernon met the man who, like the others, was reluctant to talk to a dapper, slick-looking fellow from the big city in the East. If Vernon had one quality in spades, it was charm. Eventually the man opened up and confessed that he did know of the only man in the world who could deal from the center of the deck. His name was Allen Kennedy and he lived in Pleasant Hill. The old-timer warned Vernon that even if he located the fellow it was unlikely he would discover what he was looking for because Kennedy rarely tipped his mitt. Undeterred, Vernon set out for Pleasant Hill, Missouri.

Now, the people of Pleasant Hill were just as reluctant as the gambling fraternity of Kansas City to help this stranger, particularly as he was asking questions about one of the locals. Vernon was given numerous false leads and directions. Wondering if the entire affair was a wild-goose chase, Vernon was about to give up the search. He then noticed a little girl who had dropped an ice cream cone. Vernon offered to buy her another one and then, on a whim, he asked her if she knew of a Mr. Kennedy.

Shyly, the little girl pointed to a small, white house up the street. Recounting the story years afterwards, Vernon was always fond of saying: "They say in the Scriptures, 'and a little child shall lead them,'" and so one did. Vernon knocked on the door and a soft-spoken man in overalls, about thirty-four years of age, opened the door. Vernon had found Allen Kennedy.

From the very first shuffle, Vernon knew he was in the company of a master, and although Kennedy was flattered that someone of Vernon's stature—Vernon maintained he was a big-time *mechanic* who worked the ships in the East—had come to see him, Kennedy played his cards close to the chest. Eventually, however, Kennedy placed three kings on the bottom of the pack and asked Vernon to cut the cards. Kennedy completed the cut. Everything was done according to Hoyle. Kennedy began dealing four hands of stud poker—one down and the next cards face up. Vernon watched every move. Kennedy paused and asked Vernon if he could see anything. Vernon said no. The next card Kennedy turned face up for Vernon was one of the kings. Vernon could not believe his eyes. Kennedy continued to deal at a natural, casual pace. Once again another king dropped into Vernon's hand. Kennedy finished the deal and told Vernon to turn over his hole card—the first card that had been dealt to him face down. It was the third king. Vernon had missed everything. The cards came out "as if by magic."

Although Vernon had now seen that it was possible to deal cards invisibly from the center of the deck, he still had no idea of the technique. Vernon was prepared to pay a substantial sum of money for the secret. Before offering to pay, however, he decided on a different gambit. Perhaps, Vernon thought, he might be able to show the gambler a thing or two in exchange. Vernon went through some of his repertoire and Kennedy was clearly impressed. Kennedy agreed to show Vernon the mechanics of the deal.

Vernon left Kennedy but would return a short time later, this time with his wife. First, he had some technical questions that needed clarification. Second, he wanted Kennedy to demonstrate the deal for his wife who, like many others, thought the entire notion was insane. After seeing Kennedy do the deal, she too shook her head in disbelief. Vernon practiced the deal hours each day, month after month, bringing it each time that much closer to perfection. Eventually he mastered it. Over the course of several decades he shared the technical secret with fewer than a handful of people. Charles E. Miller was one, and my mentor, Ross Bertram, was another. Finally, in 1978—forty-six years after he had first learned the technique—Vernon wrote up the technical details of the deal in his own hand and contributed it to a book on sophisticated sleight of hand by Bertram.

Vernon's life—his pursuit of information, his dedication to excellence, and his willingness to share his experience with others—has inspired thousands of people around the world. The lack of public recognition for his efforts does not diminish the effect he has had on people. If Vernon does not have the profile of Harry Houdini, it is because Vernon was a true student of *Erdnase*. Vernon knew that excessive vanity was the undoing of many experts. "To be suspected of skill," *Erdnase* points out, "is the death blow to the professional." Houdini, on the other hand, took every opportunity to enhance his reputation with the public. People found Vernon, however, intoxicating.

As Vernon's pursuit of the center deal illustrates, his energy and intellect were engaged his entire life toward perfecting his craft. Further, Vernon's magic retained its currency with each generation because he embraced the knowledge that successive generations brought to it. His natural curiosity constantly led him to new discoveries, discoveries that resulted in further advances each decade of his life. It is a testament to his legacy that most magicians, regardless of where or when they first saw Vernon, believe that they saw him at his prime. This is in stark contrast to many executives who, once they have mastered a skill, are content to recycle that expertise into a lifelong career regardless of its relevance in an ever-changing world. These people typically boast with pride the number of years they have been active in their industry, as if the quantity of time spent in business is the cash equivalent of the quality of their work. Incompetence is not the exclusive domain of the inexperienced. Advantage Players do not rest on laurels. They appreciate past accomplishments but always try to orchestrate new ones.

Despite his revered status within the magic community, Vernon always maintained that he himself was a student of magic. Of course, it takes many years of dedicated study and practice before one becomes an Advantage Player. It is a show business axiom that a successful person is a ten-year overnight sensation, a person who has struggled for many years mastering his or her craft before achieving success.

Vernon also discovered at an early age that the only things that were worth learning were things that took time to master. Christmas presents, he used to say, would come and go in a day. The satisfaction gained from acquiring a skill would last forever. As a student at Ashbury College in Ottawa, he was an accomplished diver, swimmer, hockey player, and track and field athlete. In magic, he gravitated toward sleight of hand that would take him years of practice before becoming proficient. For Vernon, practice was not arduous. It was the difficulty—the unobtainable goal—that made the pursuit—the practice of it—so enjoyable. What, however, should one practice?

An enthusiastic amateur magician once approached the great English illusionist David Devant and said, "Mr. Devant, I know three hundred tricks with cards. How many do you know?" Devant answered, "I should say that I know about eight." Devant stressed that it was better to know eight tricks thoroughly than hundreds of tricks superficially. The key is to know—really know— all of the details that create the desired *effect*. The same holds true off the stage. It is better to master a small series of skills than it is to have a superficial knowledge of a great number. Advantage Players must master few skills to be successful. These skills include problem solving, communication, time management, leadership, sales, and perhaps one or two others. Each one of these skills is like the center deal: it consists of hundreds of details each of which must be thoroughly understood and practiced if one is going to become proficient and a commercial success.

Now, mastering eight different skills is one thing,

creating a reputation that generates business is another. Once again, Vernon offered some simple but cogent advice for the Advantage Player: study one skill and practice so that you can perform it better than anyone else in the world until it becomes synonymous with your name. Everyone else's performance of that same *effect* will be compared to yours. Some Advantage Players deal the second card, others the bottom. For Allen Kennedy, it was dealing from the center of the pack. Reputation has nothing to do with originality.

Although Vernon is regarded as the seminal figure in magic, he was not known as an inventor. Vernon created his reputation by performing *effects* that were originally created by other practitioners. Each piece he performed, however, had what became known as *The Vernon Touch*—an elegance and sophistication in construction and performance. That may have been Vernon's greatest skill—perfect editorial judgment. If the magician had to perform four secret steps to achieve the desired *effect*, Vernon would analyze the effect and the methodology and then discover some way to simplify it. He would eliminate one of the steps without sacrificing the clarity of *the effect* or the directness of the method. Vernon was never satisfied with either an effect or a method. Whenever he learned something new, he would apply that knowledge to his existing—and already refined—repertoire to see if he could edit or eliminate any other steps. Magicians who marvel at the elegance and clarity of Vernon's solutions fail to realize that he developed these solutions over the course of decades. It was a lifelong pursuit. Advantage Players strive to exercise perfect editorial judgment.

Although Vernon was a poor personal correspondent, he left a rich legacy of written work. He wrote and in later years dictated a monthly column that was published over two decades. One piece of advice he gave repeatedly in his column, passed on to him originally by one of his own idols, Nate Leipzig, was "if they like you as a person, they will like what you do." It sounds so simple but remember that the obscure we see eventually but the obvious takes a little longer. Vernon was able to unlock the secret of the center deal not because he was the most gifted sleight-of-hand magician of the twentieth century but because ultimately people liked him. If he had been highhanded, curt, or obnoxious, Allen Kennedy would not have let him in the front door. Vernon remained a gentleman throughout his life.

Finally, although Vernon could be quite secretive, he was extraordinarily generous with information and advice to those who knew how to ask for it. He knew the importance of passing on information when it was needed and where it was appropriate. It is because of the spirit of his generosity that many people believe that the performance of magic has entered a new golden age.

The optimism he first displayed in *Broadway Chatter* of 1916 remained with him throughout his life. Vernon carried a list of names with him for several years prior to his death in 1992 at the age of ninety-eight. The names were of the people he considered friends or major acquaintances over the years. As one might expect, Vernon outlived virtually all of them. When one of his friends passed away, Vernon would take out the list and cross off the name. Johnny Thompson, one of the world's finest magicians, recently told me of being with Vernon when he was crossing out yet another name from his list. He asked Vernon what he was doing. Vernon—or "the Professor" as he was known in the last fifty years of his life—explained that it was a list of his friends who had passed on. Johnny looked at the Professor and then at the size of the list. He said, "I am so sorry, Professor." Vernon replied, "Don't be sorry, Johnny, I meet new friends."

Vernon was the consummate Advantage Player.

A D V A N T A G E   P L A Y

1. The chap with the goods will make good.
2. Follow your natural curiosity to discover new and arcane pieces of information.
3. Incompetence is not the exclusive domain of the inexperienced.
4. Perfect practice makes perfect. Do not reinforce bad habits.
5. Eight tricks make a master, but you must master those eight.
6. To create a reputation, master one technique better than anyone else.
7. If they like you as a person, they will like what you do.

Epilogue

*After the awakening our education pro-
gressed through close application and
constant study of the game, and the sum of
our present knowledge is proffered in this
volume, for any purpose it may answer, to
friend and foe, to the wise and the foolish, to
the good and the bad, to all alike, with but
one reservation,—that he has the price.*

S. W. ERDNASE

I
N THIS AGE OF INFORMATION there are few original
ideas that can remain a secret for long. Proprietary
knowledge is more accessible now than in any other
age. Hundreds of periodicals are published monthly and
there seems to be a never-ending flow of books for all
professions. Web sites multiply and eBay is monitored
by buyers and sellers in all categories of goods and services. One secret seems relatively safe because no one
actually knows the answer, namely who wrote *The
Expert at the Card Table*. The identity of the author has
remained a mystery for close to one hundred years
although many great minds have explored the issue.
Here is a summary of some of their findings.

In the early 1920s, a gambling aficionado from
Chicago named John Sprong tried to track down the
mysterious author of *The Expert at the Card Table*. He
contacted the publisher Frederick J. Drake and pestered

him for whatever insights he may have had of the elusive author. Drake told Sprong that Erdnase was E.S. Andrews spelled backward.

In 1946, Martin Gardner—the prolific writer of mathematics, science, magic, and skepticism who as a teenager was inspired by *Erdnase*—directed his considerable talents toward unraveling the mystery. Gardner located the illustrator of the work, Marshall D. Smith, and peppered him with questions. Although Smith was then in his seventies, he recalled meeting Erdnase, describing him as a man of slight build, not over 5'6", with soft supple hands. He guessed him to be about forty years of age. The author was quite particular about the illustrations, paid by the first check drawn on a new bank account, and confided that he was somehow related to Louis Dalrymple, a then well-known editorial cartoonist for the Democratic weekly magazine called *Puck*.

Gardner's friend, Walter B. Gibson—creator of *The Shadow* and other numerous works—suggested that Gardner speak to an old-time gambler and magician named Edgar Pratt, who claimed to have known Erdnase. In 1949, after speaking with Pratt and undertaking much detective work, Gardner and his growing number of associates tracked down a story in a San Francisco newspaper dated November 7, 1905, which detailed the suicide of Milton Franklin Andrews. This Andrews—a gambler—was one of America's most wanted, suspected of several murders, and a then-recently attempted murder. Cornered by police, Andrews apparently killed his girlfriend and then shot himself. Although the last names were similar and they shared a professional history of gambling, many doubt that Milton Franklin Andrews was the author of *The Expert at the Card Table*. The police description of Milton Franklin Andrews does not coincide with the portrait of the man described by the illustrator. Further, the 9,000 word confession letter left behind by Milton Franklin Andrews before he took his life bears little resemblance to the prose style of *The Expert at the Card Table*. Dai Vernon, for one, was not convinced. He simply would not believe that a rogue like Milton Franklin Andrews was responsible for writing the lucid and penetrating analysis of sleight of hand. In Vernon's opinion, *The Expert at the Card Table* was the product of a refined mind. Gardner stuck to his opinion, and published his theories in association with Bart Whaley and Jeff Busby in 1991 in a book entitled *The Man Who Was Erdnase*. Others, however, continued the search.

Richard Hatch of H & R Magic Books has been one of the most tireless sleuths. His searching of census data and records in the Library of Congress has turned up two other prospective candidates. The first is James Dewitt Andrews. Born in 1856 and an author of numerous treatises published in Chicago between 1884 and 1910, this Andrews was not only an attorney but also a professor of law on the faculty at Northwestern University between 1895 and 1897, and a post-graduate Professor of Jurisprudence at Chicago Law School thereafter. He resided in Chicago between 1891 until 1903, when he moved to New York City. He died in New York in 1928, two years before the American copyright in the book would have come up for renewal.

For those who do not believe S. W. Erdnase is E. S. Andrews spelled backward, Richard Hatch offers one other potential candidate. His name is Edwin Sumner Andrews, a salesman for the Chicago & Northwestern Railroad who had worked in the railroad industry—a breeding ground for Advantage Players— since boyhood.

David Alexander—another *Erdnase* scholar, professional detective, and author of *Star Trek Creator: The Authorized Biography of Gene Roddenberry*—has taken a different approach to solving the riddle. Ignoring the conventional approach suggested by the backward spelling of S. W. Erdnase, Alexander first developed a profile for the type of person who would be capable of authoring such a work.

> *The profile is a university-educated Northerner with extensive writing experience from a wealthy family, engaged in a profession that demands an analytical mind and possibly, or probably, writing skills, who practices amateur magic and harbors a secret fascination with card table artifice.**

Alexander expanded the analysis of the name S. W. Erdnase and concluded that it was a complex rather than a simple anagram that could result in at least four different proper names other than E. S. Andrews: Ward Essen, Wes Anders, E. W. Sanders, and W. E. Sanders. His detective work led to Wilbur Edgerton Sanders, the son of a wealthy and politically active family from Montana. Sanders was educated in the northeast of America and became a mining engineer, traveling

---

* Alexander, David, "The Magician As Detective—New Light On Erdnase," *Genii*, Vol. 63, No. 1, January, 2000, Washington, D.C., p. 21.

around frontier towns and mining camps in the West before settling in Berkeley, California, in 1921. He died in 1935.

The *New York Times Magazine* on December 3, 2000, was dedicated to secrets—interestingly enough none of which concerned Advantage Players. Luc Sante in "What Secrets Tell" wrote:

> *People need secrets because they need the assurance that there is something left to discover, that they have not exhausted the limits of their environment, that a prize might lie in wait like money in the pocket of an old jacket, that the existence of things beyond their ken might propose a corollary that their own minds contain unsuspected corridors. People need uncertainty and security. It's not that secrets make them feel small but that they make the world seem bigger—a major necessity these days, when sensations need to be extreme to register at all. Secrets reawaken that feeling from childhood that the ways of the world were infinitely mysterious, unpredictable and densely packed, and that someday you might come to know and master them. Secrets purvey affordable glamor, suggest danger without presenting an actual threat. If there were no more secrets, an important motor of life would be stopped, and the days would merge into a continuous blur. Secrets hold out the promise, false but necessary, that death will be deferred until their unveiling.***

S. W. Erdnase could not have said it any better.

** Sante, Luc, "What Secrets Tell," *The New York Times Magazine*, Section 6, December 3, 2000, *The New York Times*, New York, p. 77.

Advantage Charts

A. The Mechanics of Problem Solving

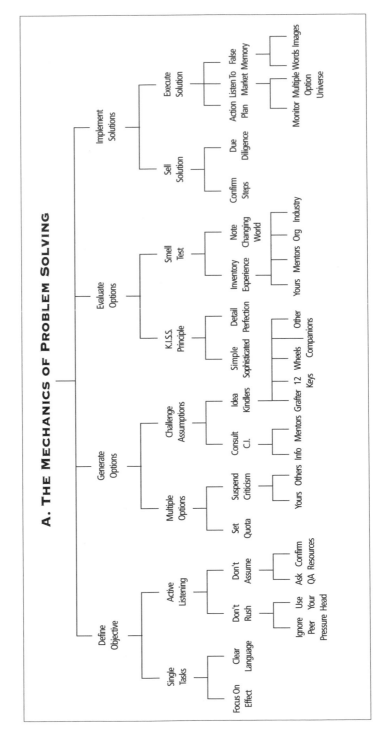

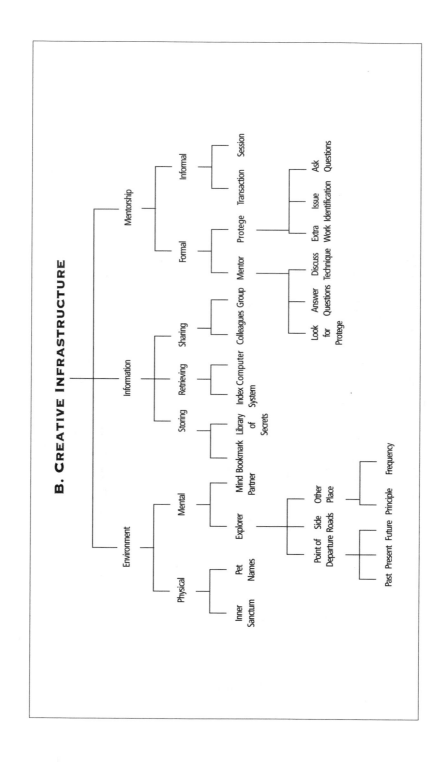

B. CREATIVE INFRASTRUCTURE

C. FORGING THE FUTURE

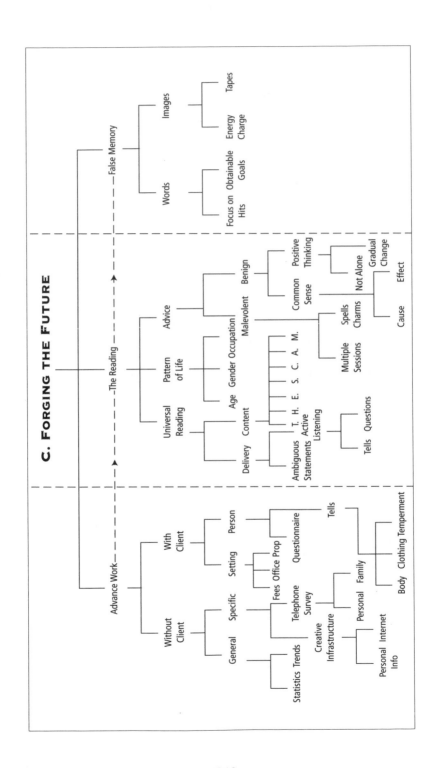

Advantage Words

Advantage Play—an effective and legal advantage over the competition based on principles of deception.

Creative Infrastructure—an organized repository of personal and professional resources that create an inventory of experience from which you can generate ideas and evaluate options.

Idea Kindlers—techniques that help challenge assumptions and develop insight into difficult problems. Often the key to unlocking the subconscious.

Information Anxiety—a term coined by the futurist Richard Saul Wurman that describes the anxiety one feels at being overwhelmed by information.

Inner Sanctum—a positive environment for creative problem solving.

Multiple Option Universe—an inventory of solutions developed during the second stage of The Mechanics of Problem Solving, of which each option will achieve the same effect—the solution to the problem.

Point of Departure—the starting point for the creative journey that reveals much about the final destination and the path to it.

Principles of Deception—the theoretical base for problem solving in the real world.

Rainmaker—a person who generates a significant amount of work or business for the enterprise because of a well-developed and trusted sense of smell.

Sleight of Mind—a technique that is based on the performer's capacity for management rather than his or her digital dexterity.

Strategic Selling—a sales system advocated by Stephen E. Heiman and Diane Sanchez in their best-selling book of the same name.

Technology Anxiety—the fear of not coping with or capitalizing on the opportunity that technology presents.

Tells—inconsistencies in action or appearance that telegraph technique and dilute the impact of the effect.

The Impossible—a problem waiting to be solved.

The Mechanic—a person who is able to direct the course of play by dealing the winning hand to a secret ally.

The Mechanics of Problem Solving—a four-step common sense approach to problem solving.

The Other Place—a repository of principles inherent in nature that, once discovered and applied, can make any problem disappear.

The Real Work—a term used by Advantage Players to describe the most refined and sophisticated techniques that convert a good trick into a miracle or a secret sleight into something that *gets the money*.

T.H.E. S.C.A.M.—areas that concern most people—travel, health, expectations, sex, career, ambition, and money—as they move through life.

The Vernon Touch—a style of performance that epitomizes economy of movement, confidence, and grace.

Universal Read—a profile of the client's past, present, and future delivered in general terms but interpreted by the client as pertinent or appropriate to just them.

Advantage
Favorites

THE LITERATURE ON MAGIC, creativity, psychic readings, Advantage Play, and sales is vast. Each subject is a separate discipline that commands its own extensive reading list. The following titles represent some of my personal favorites. Some are difficult to find because they are out of print or are available through private channels. The best source is www.magicbookshop.com. Other references are perennial favorites available in inexpensive paperback editions at most major bookstores. All are worthy of your consideration.

On Erdnase

Erdnase, S. W., *The Expert at the Card Table*, Dover Publications
This book remains the fountainhead for Advantage Play and every serious student of magic. Even after one hundred years, the book retains its currency. Challenging, inspirational, and entertaining, it requires study, application, and more study.

Gardner, Martin, and Smith, Marshall, *The Gardner-Smith Correspondence*, H & R Magic Books, Humble, Texas, 1999

This small booklet reproduces the correspondence between 1946 and 1953 of Martin Gardner and the illustrator of *The Expert at the Card Table*. A must-have for anyone planning on joining the hunt for the elusive S. W. Erdnase. The correspondence is accompanied by an introduction by Martin Gardner in which he provides what are perhaps his final thoughts on this fascinating subject.

Ortiz, Darwin, *The Annotated Erdnase*, A Magical Publication, Pasadena, California, 1991

A superb work produced by one of the world's leading authorities on casino gambling, Advantage Play, and magic. It is the definitive study on the technical aspects of *The Expert at the Card Table*. A must for any true student of Erdnase.

Sawyer, Thomas A., *S. W. Erdnase: Another View*, Second Edition, Thomas A. Sawyer, Tustin, California, 1997

Lawyer, magic historian, and bibliographer reviews the evidence presented by Erdnase historians and, in particular, the work presented in *The Man Who Was Erdnase* (see below) to provide a sober second thought on the identity and publication history of *The Expert at the Card Table*.

Vernon, Dai, *Revelations*, A Magical Publication, Pasadena, California, 1984

Written between 1959 and 1961, Vernon's manuscript remained closely guarded until being released to the magic community in 1984. Although Vernon's annotations and comments are terse in comparison to Darwin Ortiz's in *The Annotated Erdnase*, no one could be considered an expert on *The Expert* until he or she has explored Vernon's commentary. *Revelations* also contains a brilliant introduction by MacArthur Foundation recipient, Stanford University professor, and student of Vernon, Persi Diaconis.

Whaley, Bart, and Gardner, Martin, and Busby, Jeff, *The Man Who Was Erdnase***, Jeff Busby Magic, Inc., Oakland, California, 1991**

A groundbreaking examination of the life of S. W. Erdnase, revealing for the first time the history of S. W. Erdnase as Milton Franklin Andrews, one of the most wanted criminals in America. Based on the extensive research conducted by Martin Gardner and augmented by the penetrating insights of Bart Whaley and Jeff Busby, this book is a scholarly account of the author, the technical nuances, and publication history of *The Expert at the Card Table*.

On Advantage Play

Marks, Dustin D., *Cheating at Blackjack and Advantage Play***, Index Publishing Group, Inc., San Diego, California, 1994**

A must read for anyone looking for *the real work* on defrauding a casino. Frank and informative, it is guaranteed to open the eyes of anyone who has ever gambled in, visited, or worked in a casino.

Marks, Dustin D., *Cheating at Blackjack Squared***, Index Publishing Group, Inc., San Diego, California, 1996**

A companion volume to *Cheating at Blackjack and Advantage Play*, this book is a definitive resource on how Advantage Players cheat at Blackjack and other card games. It covers switching cards in play, stacking the deck, and stealing chips as well as how computers and other sophisticated electronic devices can help the Advantage Player *get the money.*

Ortiz, Darwin, *Gambling Scams*, **Dodd, Mead & Company, New York, 1984**
A lucid explanation of up-to-date sleight-of-hand moves for manipulating cards and dice as well as mechanical gadgets and psychological ploys used by crooked gamblers and casinos. Written by Darwin Ortiz (See *The Annotated Erdnase)*, highly recommended for anyone with even a passing interest in gambling.

Ortiz, Darwin, *Darwin Ortiz On Casino Gambling— The Complete Guide To Playing And Winning*, **Dodd, Mead & Company, New York, 1986**
A clear, comprehensive, and authoritative guide to casino gambling offering strategy, drills, and exercises, all of which are legal and above board. This book also discusses all aspects of casino operations including credit policies, junket programs, casino promotions, gambling systems, and casino etiquette.

Prus, Robert C., and Sharper, C.R.D., *Road Hustler—Grifting, Magic, and the Thief Subculture*, **Expanded Edition, Kaufman and Greenberg, New York, 1991**
An ethnocentric account of career contingencies of Advantage Players assembled and prepared by university professor Robert Prus in association with one of his students, a gambler trying to re-educate himself toward

a more reputable career. A unique publication, one that has become the textbook of impression management for Advantage Players.

On Creativity

Claxton, Guy, *Hare Brain, Tortoise Mind*, Fourth Estate, London, 1997

This book suggests that there are other modes of problem solving that are equally or more effective in certain circumstances than our default mode (D-mode), which prefers reasonable, purposeful, and precise thinking. Specifically, the author suggests that we should learn to trust our unconscious mind to do the thinking for us. I believe such thinking has its place in creative problem solving. It is important, however, to understand the technique of tapping the unconscious within *The Mechanics of Problem Solving.*

de Bono, Edward, *Lateral Thinking—A Textbook of Creativity*, Penguin Books, England, 1970

One of the best books by the guru of lateral thinking, this pioneering work should be required reading for anyone interested in expanding the brain's capacity for challenging assumptions. It also serves as a useful introduction to the de Bono oeuvre.

Michalko, Michael, *Thinkertoys—A Handbook of Business Creativity For the 90s*, Ten Speed Press, Berkeley, California, 1991

An excellent source of thirty techniques and hundreds of hints that can help generate ideas in a business environment. More pragmatic than most books exploring idea generation, it offers useful techniques for brainstorming and overcoming mental blocks to creativity.

Wurman, Richard Saul, *Informationanxiety2*, QUE, Indianapolis, Indiana, 2001

An expanded and updated version of *Information Anxiety*, a classic guide to comprehending and communicating information. Essential reading for Advantage Players, particularly those who want to build a *Creative Infrastructure* and harness its potential.

On Sales

Heiman, Stephen E., and Sanchez, Diane, *The New Strategic Selling*, Revised Edition, Warner Books, New York, 1998

As mentioned in Chapter 7, I believe this to be the most informative and practical published guide to selling. A must read.

On Cold Reading

Jones, Bascom, *King of the Cold Readers*, Bascom Jones, Bakersfield, California, 1989

Considered a masterwork for those in the know, this book disclosed, at the time of its publication, the most up-to-date pseudo-psychic techniques for advanced professionals. Although ten years have passed since its original publication, it remains a cornerstone text for the profession.

Nelson, Robert A., *The Art of Cold Reading*, **Revised Edition, Micky Hades Enterprises, Calgary, Alberta, 1971**

This work is considered a pioneering work outlining professional techniques for psychics and mentalists. The language and the examples may be dated, but the principles resonate as clearly today as they must have when the book was originally published in 1951.

Nelson, Robert A., *A Sequel To The Art of Cold Reading*, **Micky Hades Enterprises, Calgary, Alberta, 1971**

Further insight and technique for professional psychics by a pivotal figure in the profession. (See above.)

Saville, Thomas K., and Dewey, Herb, *Red Hot Cold Reading*, **1984**

A professor of psychology joined forces with a psychic-reader, mentalist and hypnotist to provide a more up-to-date analysis of the technical and psychological aspects of cold reading.

On Stewart James

James, Stewart, *Stewart James In Print: The First Fifty Years*, **edited by P. Howard Lyons and Allan Slaight, Jogesta Ltd, Toronto, Ontario, 1989**

A magnum opus reproducing hundreds of tricks published by Stewart James in various books and journals over a fifty-year span augmented by Stewart's own recollections of his life and his particular approach to the creative. Superseded only by *The James File* (See below.)

Slaight, Allan, *The James File*, Jogesta Ltd, Toronto, Ontario, 2000
Five hundred and fifty-six previously unpublished originations by Stewart James and variations of his published works by many of the magicians he inspired meticulously compiled and written by Allan Slaight, the definitive authority on Stewart James and his mode of thinking. A monumental work in the history of magic.

On Dai Vernon

Vernon, Dai, *He Fooled Houdini: Dai Vernon A Magical Life*, edited by Bruce Cervon and Keith Burns, L & L Publishing, Tahoma, California, 1992
This book is an autobiographical account of Dai Vernon prepared by Bruce Cervon and Keith Burns from transcripts of recorded interviews that Richard Buffum, a California newspaperman and amateur magician, made with Vernon in 1965. There are many wonderful anecdotes and, for now, it remains the most complete account of his life.

Vernon wrote or contributed magic to dozens of publications over the course of his rich artistic life. Most of these books have been published or are being republished by L & L Publications. If you are interested in learning more of Vernon's magic, you will find a way to track down this publisher and these publications.

Acknowledgments

ALTHOUGH I HAVE TRIED TO GIVE the book a singular voice, I must acknowledge the many people who have shaped my thought and life over the years, particularly with regard to *Advantage Play*. I owe more than a significant debt of gratitude to Ross Bertram, Bob Farmer, P. Howard Lyons, Brian J. Arnold, Allan Slaight, and Patrick Watson.

I would also like to thank the many other people who have offered me encouragement and advice over the years including Pat Lyons, Ray Massecar, Tom Ransom, Mel Stover, Karl Johnson and the magicians, gamblers, and psychics who have shared with me some of their innermost secrets. To Suleyman Fattah for his preliminary illustrations and Toivo Kiil for his editorial assistance. A special thank you to David Lavin and Anna Porter for their unbridled enthusiasm for my work.

To Edward and Derek Verner for allowing me to explore without restriction the life and work of their father. To Stewart James for inviting me in off the porch. To my wife and children who probably still do not know how to describe what exactly it is that I do for a living.

And to S. W. Erdnase—whoever you may be.

The Author

D AVID BEN IS THE SOLE PROTÉGÉ of Ross Bertram—
one of the great sleight-of-hand magicians of
the twentieth century—from whom he learned the intri-
cacies of *The Expert at the Card Table*. As a magician
David has performed throughout the United States,
Canada, England and in Mexico, France and Japan. He
is the co-creator, performer and producer of *The
Conjuror* and *The Conjuror's Suite*—critically acclaimed
theatrical performances that have been staged at pre-
miere venues and theater festivals and enjoyed long
commercial runs in Toronto, Canada, and other centers.
David has appeared on dozens of television programs
and was the subject of the documentary film "A
Conjuror in the Making," which obtained the highest
seasonal ratings for *Adrienne Clarkson Presents* when
aired on the CBC in Canada. The film also aired on
Breakfast in the Arts on the Arts and Entertainment
Channel (A&E) in the United States.

A graduate of the University of Toronto, the
University of Western Ontario, and the London School
of Economics, David was a tax lawyer with the international law firm Goodman, Phillips and Vineberg. He
started the trend referred to in the *Wall Street Journal* as
"the magician as motivational speaker" in 1990, and
remains in great demand as a corporate keynote speaker

on creativity, problem solving, and sales. His clientele include IBM, Standard Radio Inc., Bell Canada, National Trust, Arthur Andersen, Imperial Oil, Scotiabank, Ernst & Young, Minolta, and the Gemological Institute of America. He has designed and presented interactive trade show presentations for such clients as 3M, Amdalh, and Toshiba.

David has also been the consultant on several television documentaries: "The Wizards of Awe"—the highest rated two-part documentary in the history of CBC's *The Journal*; the Daniel Zuckerbrot film "Martin Gardner Mathemagician" for *The Nature of Things*; and History Television's "Dai Vernon—The Spirit of Magic" (in which he also acted as associate producer). This film is the recipient of many awards including the Chris Award from the Columbus Film Festival, where it was also selected for its prestigious showcase as the best documentary biography produced in the year; Bronze Award at Worldfest, Texas; and as a finalist in the New York Film Festival. Since working on the Dai Vernon film, David has become the official biographer of Dai Vernon and the legal representative of the Dai Vernon Estate within the magic community. David acted as consultant for investigative journalist Karl Johnson's article for *American Heritage* on Dai Vernon's pursuit of the legendary middle deal and for History Television's "The Life and Strange Genius of Stewart James." He was also featured as on-camera guest in John Fisher's superb documentary "Heroes of Magic" for Pearson Television, England.

David is the founder of Magicana—a not-for-profit corporation dedicated to the pursuit, study, and development of magic as a performing art. He is the recent recipient of a U.S. Green Card as an "alien of extraordinary artistic merit" and now divides his time between residences in New York City and Toronto. For more information visit www.davidben.com

Index